Experiencing the Mingling of God with Man for the Oneness of the Body of Christ

Witness Lee

Living Stream Ministry

Anaheim, CA • www.lsm.org

First Edition, May 2004.

ISBN 0-7363-2597-2

Published by

Living Stream Ministry
2431 W. La Palma Ave., Anaheim, CA 92801 U.S.A.
P. O. Box 2121, Anaheim, CA 92814 U.S.A.

Printed in the United States of America

04   05   06   07   08   09   10   /   9   8   7   6   5   4   3   2   1

CONTENTS

PREFACE

This book is composed of twelve messages given by Brother Witness Lee in March of 1963 in New York City, New York. Each weekend, beginning with March 8-10 and ending with March 29-31, three messages were given. These messages were not reviewed by the speaker.

CHAPTER ONE

APPLYING CHRIST AS LIFE IN OUR DAILY LIFE

Scripture Reading: John 1:4, 1, 14, 17-18; 4:14; 5:39-40; 6:35, 53-57, 63; Col. 1:12; 2:16-17

The ministry of the apostle John has a special place among the ministries of the apostles, and among all the books of the Bible, his books have a special or particular nature. In these first few messages we would like to consider the Gospel of John, which has three main points—Christ as life, the increase of Christ, and the oneness of the increase of Christ. In this message we will examine the first point, concerning Christ as life.

GOD'S ETERNAL INTENTION

The entire Bible and the Gospel of John in particular reveal to us that God's eternal intention is to work Himself into us and be mingled with us so that we may have Him as our life and that He may be expressed through us. This is what is eternally in the mind of God. In order to accomplish this intention, the Lord Jesus came to us as the Word of God so that we could receive Him and take Him as our life. Christ as the Word of God is the definition, explanation, expression, and manifestation of God (1:1). Furthermore, all the fullness of the Godhead, which is all that God is, dwells in Him bodily (Col. 2:9). Thus, Christ is not only the expression of God but also the embodiment of God. When we receive Christ, we receive God Himself as everything to us.

When Christ comes into us, He brings God Himself as grace and reality into us. John 1:17 says that "grace and reality came through Jesus Christ." Grace is commonly defined as something given to us by others or something we gain from others free of charge. However, real grace is God received and gained by us. The apostle Paul tells us that everything in the universe is refuse and that only God Himself is grace to us (Phil. 3:8; 2 Tim. 4:22). The Lord Jesus brought God to us so that we might gain and receive the true grace in the universe, which is God Himself. When we experience and realize God as grace, He becomes reality to us. God gained by us is grace, and God realized, experienced, and enjoyed by us is reality.

KNOWING THE PRACTICAL WAY
TO TAKE CHRIST AS OUR LIFE

How can we gain God as grace and experience and realize God as reality? The book of John tells us that the simplest way for us to gain and experience God is to take Christ as our life. The Lord made this matter simple by telling us that He is the bread of life for us to eat and the living water for us to drink (6:35; 4:10; 7:37). Thus, if we want to gain and experience God, we must take Christ as our life by eating Christ as our food and drinking Christ as our drink. We may know the doctrine that Christ is the bread of life, but do we know how to actually take Christ as the bread of life into us? Do we know the real and practical way to apply Christ as life to our daily living and take Him as our food and drink? This matter sounds simple. However, I have discovered that although most of the Lord's children know that Christ is life and that He is the bread of life, they do not know the practical way to take Christ as their bread, and they do not have the experience of Christ as life. Although the way to experience, apply, and appropriate Christ in daily life is very simple, most of the Lord's children do not know the way. Thus, there is a need among the Lord's children to know the way to take Christ as life.

In these messages I do not want to present mere doctrines, because our need is not for mere doctrines. Rather, our need is to know how to take Christ as life in an experiential and practical way. Our physical eating and drinking are very practical matters. Likewise, the Lord being the bread of life and the water of life to us are very practical matters and not mere doctrines. We may know the doctrines, but we may not practice applying and appropriating Christ in our daily living. If I were to ask you how many meals you have each day, you would probably say that you have three meals— breakfast, lunch, and dinner. However, if I were to ask you how many times you had taken Christ as your life today, you would probably give me an uncertain answer. Every day we should be very certain that we have experienced Christ as our daily bread. Every day we should be able to point out to the angels and the enemy the number of times we enjoyed Christ, just as we are able to say how many meals we take each day.

EXPERIENCING CHRIST
AS THE REALITY OF EVERY POSITIVE THING

In order to enjoy Christ in a practical way, we must realize that all the positive physical and material things that we enjoy are not the real things but only shadows and figures that point to the real thing, which is Christ Himself. Do you think that the light in your house is the real light? If you are not enjoying Christ, you may be in the light of your house, yet you may actually be in darkness, because this light is not the real light. It is only a shadow or figure pointing to the real light, which is Christ (1:4; 9:5). If we have Christ, we have light, and if we do not have Christ, we do not have light. Likewise, the food and water we take in every day are not the real food and water. They are shadows, showing us that we need to take in the real food and water, which are Christ Himself. When I travel to different places, I often stay in the homes of the saints. However, those homes are not my real home. My real home, or dwelling place, is Christ. Moses realized this, saying in Psalm 90:1, "O Lord, You have been our dwelling place / In all generations." Sometimes when I am traveling by airplane, I tell the Lord, "Lord, I am not in this plane. I am in You. You are my plane, my hiding place, and my dwelling place." We must realize that all these material things are shadows pointing to the real thing, which is Christ Himself (Col. 2:16-17).

While you are breathing, do you realize that the air you are breathing is not the real air? The real air is Christ Himself

(John 20:22). We must constantly breathe Christ day by day. We cannot stop breathing, because once we stop, we are dead. Thus, we must breathe Christ all the time. Often while I am walking along the street, I tell the Lord, "Lord, this street is not my real way. You are my real way; You are the way to me. If I do not have You, I do not have the way, but when I have You, I have the way" (14:6). When we are putting on our clothes in the morning, we should realize that our clothes are not the real clothes. Our real clothing is Christ (Gal. 3:27). We should pray to the Lord, "Lord, these clothes are not my real clothes. You are my real clothing. These clothes are nothing but a shadow. You are the reality of these clothes. I praise You and thank You that You are my covering and clothing. I may be putting on this outward clothing, but in my heart I am putting on You." This is the way to apply Christ while we are putting on our clothing. Even when we are drinking a beverage, we must tell the Lord, "I do not merely wish to be refreshed by this beverage; I wish to be refreshed by You. Lord, You are my real refreshment" (cf. John 4:14; 7:37). We all must experience and apply Christ in such a practical way. We should not merely learn doctrines and listen to teachings about Christ. Rather, we must experience Christ as our daily necessities and our life supply day by day and even moment by moment.

The Lord told us, "He who eats Me, he also shall live because of Me" (6:57). We need to eat the Lord so that we will live by Him. We have a natural life, but this is not the real life by which we live before God. It is only a shadow that points to the real life, which is Christ Himself (11:25; 14:6; 1 John 5:12; 1 Tim. 6:19). Today are we living by our own life or by Christ as our life? In order to live by Christ as our life, we must forsake, deny, and reject our own life and take Christ as our real life day by day and moment by moment (Matt. 16:24-25; Col. 3:4). When we are going to visit a friend, we must remember not to do it by our natural life but by Christ as our life. While I am speaking the word, in the depth of my heart I am trusting in the Lord, not in myself. I speak not by my natural man or my natural life but by Christ as my life. In a sense, we still must live a natural, human life. However, we must realize that the real life by which we live before God is not the natural life but Christ Himself as life to us. We must realize that our physical life and all the positive material things around us are only shadows; they are not the reality. The reality is Christ Himself.

Do you realize that your eyes are not the real eyes? The real eyes are Christ Himself. If we do not have Christ, we are blind. Only when we have Christ are we able to see everything through Christ, by Christ, and in Christ (Luke 4:18; John 9:6-7; Rev. 3:18). Do you realize that even your Bible, though it is the Word of God, is only the written Word of God? The real, living Word is Christ Himself. In John 5:39-40 the Lord told the Pharisees, "You search the Scriptures, because you think that in them you have eternal life....Yet you are not willing to come to Me that you may have life." Many people come to the Bible without coming to Christ. They contact the written Word but do not contact the living Word, which is Christ. When we come to the Scriptures, we should pray, "Lord, You are the real Word. I come to contact You through the written Word. You are the living Word and the real Word, and through the written Word I can contact You as the living and real Word."

Colossians 2:16-17 says, "Let no one therefore judge you in eating and in drinking or in respect of a feast or of a new moon or of the Sabbath, which are a shadow of the things to come, but the body is of Christ." Eating, drinking, the feasts, the new moon, and the Sabbath are all shadows of Christ as the reality. The new moon is a figure of Christ as our new and fresh start. Day by day Christ is a new start to us when we enjoy Him. We can have a new moon, a new start, not just once a month but every day and even every moment. The Sabbath is a figure of Christ as our rest. As long as we enjoy Christ as our rest, we may have a Sabbath not only on the Lord's Day but also every day and every hour. The feasts, the eating, and the drinking reveal Christ as our enjoyment. We should have a feast not merely once every three months or on holidays; we should have a feast moment by moment by enjoying Christ. If we want to have a new start, have rest, or experience enjoyment as in a feast, we must apply and appropriate Christ.

THE ENJOYMENT OF CHRIST
SOLVING ALL OUR PROBLEMS

Many of our problems can be solved by taking Christ as the solution to our problems. Often when people come to talk to me, they tell me only the negative side of their situation. Some have come to me, saying, "Brother Lee, I cannot control my temper. I lose my temper so easily." Others have told me, "Brother Lee, my experience with the Lord is not very stable. Sometimes I am very much with the Lord, but later I fall away from the Lord." No doubt it is difficult to overcome sin, give up the world, and forsake the worldly things. There are many matters like these on the negative side. However, I have discovered that there is no need to talk about these negative things. I have pointed this out to many of the Lord's children, saying, "Brothers and sisters, forget about the negative things. Let us go on positively by taking Christ, experiencing Christ, applying Christ, and exercising to appropriate Christ moment by moment in our daily living." If we do not eat and drink enough, we may eventually be infected with germs and may cause ourselves much trouble. Thus, instead of paying attention to the germs on the negative side, we should forget about them and focus on eating and drinking properly on the positive side. Then all the negative troubles will be solved by our positive enjoyment. We must enjoy Christ in a positive way.

It is strange that although we have such a rich supply, most of the time we do not enjoy it. Instead, we spend our time and energy trying to deal with the negative things. I have met many sisters who told me that they were very frustrated because they were unable to be patient with their children or their husband. I told them that there was no need for them to be patient. Do you realize that the Lord is not asking us to be patient? Rather, He is asking us to enjoy Him and apply Him in our daily life. If we take Christ as our life and eat and drink Him, we will realize that it is easy to be patient. We may even be patient without knowing it.

Christ is everything to us. He is our understanding and

our wisdom (1 Cor. 1:30). He is our release and our limitation. Christ is our kingdom, our home, and our dwelling place. He is a sphere and a realm to us. Day by day we are walking in Christ (Col. 2:6). However, we must not be satisfied with simply knowing these things as doctrines. Do we truly know how to enjoy Christ as our daily bread and our living water? Do we have the experience of appropriating Christ in all our daily affairs? Do we truly realize that Christ is our dwelling place, our way, our clothing, our rest, our joy, and our wisdom? This is the problem with most Christians today; they have many teachings but too little experience.

Today there are many doctrines and teachings among the Lord's children, yet when you ask them how to experience Christ in a real way, very few are able to answer. I am very burdened by this matter. There is such an urgent need that the Lord's children know Christ in a practical and experiential way, not a doctrinal way. In these messages I am not teaching mere doctrine, because many of us may know that Christ is our life, the bread of life, the living water, and everything to us. What I am pointing out is our need for practical experience. We need to ask ourselves how much we experience Christ in our daily living and apply Him in our daily situations. The Lord told us that He is the bread of life and the living water (John 6:48; 4:10). Bread and water are simple matters, but they are also very practical. We should not take these things as mere doctrines; rather, we should practice them day by day in a real way. This is to be a real Christian. A Christian is one who enjoys and applies Christ all the time. I hope that we all would spend some time to consider this matter and to tell the Lord, "Lord, I realize that You are everything to me, but I want to prove this in my daily experience. I do not want to tell people what You are by merely giving them teachings and doctrines. I want to be able to testify how You are everything to me. I want to apply You to all the affairs in my daily life moment by moment."

THE WAY TO APPLY CHRIST AS OUR LIFE

If we are going to apply Christ as our life, we must know what Christ is. When some people heard that Christ was the bread of life and that He could be their food, they said, "This word is hard; who can hear it?" (6:60). They could not understand how this man could give Himself as bread to them and be eaten by them, so they left Him. However, the Lord told the disciples, "It is the Spirit who gives life;...the words which I have spoken to you are spirit and are life" (v. 63). In order to apply Christ as our life, we must understand the relationship between the word and the Spirit.

We have the written Word, the Bible, in our hand and Christ as the Spirit in our spirit. In other words, we have the Holy Scriptures outwardly and the Holy Spirit inwardly. Whenever we contact the written Word not merely with our mind but with our spirit, the word spoken to us by the Lord becomes the Spirit to us. Outwardly, the written Word is still the Word, but when we receive the written Word with our spirit, the word received by us becomes the Spirit in us. When we speak what we have received to someone else, the Spirit in us becomes the word again, and when that person receives the word, the word becomes the Spirit in him. We must always contact the Word by exercising our spirit. When we contact the Word with our spirit, we receive the word, and the word becomes the Spirit in us (Eph. 6:17-18). Because this very Spirit is life to us, we feel living, refreshed, satisfied, and strengthened. We sense that we are alive because we have the life supply. This life also becomes light to us (John 1:4). Because we not only have the life but are also in the light, we sense that we are clear. When we have the word, we have the Spirit; when we have the Spirit, we enjoy life; and when we enjoy life, we experience the light. This is the way to walk in Christ, live by Christ, and apply Christ in everything. We must not merely listen to messages and learn doctrines. Instead, we must learn how to contact the written Word with our spirit. When we contact the Word with our spirit, we receive the word into us, and the word becomes the living Spirit within us. This living Spirit then becomes life to us, and we sense that we are satisfied, strengthened, refreshed, and living. We also sense that our whole being is in the light.

Christ is a sphere, a realm, in which we can walk, live, work, and have our daily life. In this realm we can experience and enjoy Christ as the allotted portion of the saints in the light (Col. 1:12). This light is a sphere or realm, just as darkness is also a sphere or realm. This light is a kingdom of light; when we walk within this kingdom of light, we are controlled and ruled by the light. This light is the life, this life is the Spirit, and the Spirit is the word, which is Christ Himself. Thus, we must take Christ as the living word. When we take the word, it becomes the Spirit within us, and this very Spirit is the life supply to us. As we enjoy the life supply, the life becomes light to us—a realm, sphere, and kingdom of light in which we may walk, work, and live.

We need to realize our need to apply Christ in our daily life. We need to practice contacting Christ and applying Christ day by day and moment by moment. If we are going to be real Christians, we must exercise to experience, apply, appropriate, and enjoy Christ as our spiritual portion all the time. If we have this kind of experience, we will become the increase of Christ, and when we become the increase of Christ, we will see the oneness of the increase of Christ (John 3:29-30). In the Gospel of John there are three main points— life, the increase, and the oneness. Christ as the embodiment of God is life to us, and when we enjoy and experience Him as our life, we become His increase, which must be one.

CHAPTER TWO

THE INCREASE OF CHRIST
AND THE ONENESS OF THE INCREASE

Scripture Reading: John 3:29-30; 12:24-25; 15:5; 17:21-23; 20:17;
1 Cor. 10:16-17; 12:12-13

THE CHURCH AS THE INCREASE OF CHRIST

We have pointed out that the three main points in the
Gospel of John are life, the increase, and the oneness of the
increase. The Gospel of John tells us that the Lord Jesus
came to give us life and that this life is Himself (10:10b; 14:6).
Christ Himself is life to us, so when we receive Christ, we
receive life. The purpose of this life is to produce the bride,
who is the increase of Christ. In 3:29-30 John the Baptist
said, "He who has the bride is the bridegroom; but the friend
of the bridegroom, who stands and hears him, rejoices with
joy because of the bridegroom's voice. This joy of mine therefore is made full. He must increase, but I must decrease." The
bridegroom is Christ, and the bride, the increase of Christ, is
the church, which comprises all those who believe in Christ.

The picture of Adam and Eve in Genesis indicates that
the church is the bride and the increase of Christ. It shows us
that Eve was not only Adam's bride but also Adam's increase.
God did not create Adam and Eve apart from each other.
Rather, God first created Adam and then took a rib from Adam
in order to make Eve as a counterpart for him (2:22). Thus,
Eve was a part of Adam; she was both the counterpart and the
increase of Adam. Without Eve, Adam would have been single
like a bachelor, but with Eve, Adam had a wife and a counterpart to match him. Similarly, by Himself Christ is single and
needs a bride. This bride is the church, which is also the

increase of Christ. The church came out of Christ, just as Eve came out of Adam, and the church is the same as Christ in life and in nature (2 Pet. 1:4), just as Eve was the same as Adam in life and in nature. Thus, the church is the increase of Christ.

The One Grain Becoming the Many Grains

The Gospel of John reveals that the Lord came to impart life to us in order that He could have an increase for Himself. In 12:24-25 the Lord told us that He was the one grain of wheat that would fall into the earth to die in order to become the many grains. Originally, He was the one grain of wheat, but through death and resurrection He became the many grains, which are the believers as the increase of Christ, the multiplication of the one grain. As the many grains we are exactly the same as the original grain, Christ. In our natural life we are the increase and multiplication of Adam, but as those who have been reborn, we have the life of Christ, and because of this divine life, we are the increase and multiplication of Christ. In the natural realm we are of Adam, but in the spiritual realm we are of Christ. We must clearly realize that in the spirit we are Christ's increase.

If we realize what the life and nature of the church are, we will realize the purpose and function of the church. The church as the Body of Christ is nothing but Christ Himself (1 Cor. 12:12). The church is the increase of Christ, and we are members of the church; thus, we are members of Christ (Rom. 12:5). When we were regenerated, we became members of Christ, and now Christ must be the life by which we live.

We must learn to always deny our natural life in order to live by Christ as our life. This must not be a mere doctrine and teaching to us; it must also be our practice and experience. For instance, suppose a brother comes to speak to us. By which life and in which person would we contact him? As Christians we have two lives and two persons. We have two lives; one is the life of Adam, and the other is Christ as our life (Col. 3:4). We have two persons; on the one hand, Adam is our person, and on the other hand, Christ is our person (Phil. 1:21a). Because we have two lives and two persons, we may say that we have two last names; our last name was originally Adam, but now it is Christ. Whenever we are going to talk with someone, we must realize and remember that we are two persons with two lives. We are constantly in a situation in which we must choose to live by one life or the other and in one person or the other. Thus, we must constantly look to the Lord that we may choose to contact people and do everything in the new man and by the new, spiritual life rather than by the old man and by the old, natural life.

Living in Christ and by Christ as our life involves the lesson of the cross. It is a fact that our old man has been crucified on the cross (Rom. 6:6), but when we are contacting people, we must apply the crucifixion of the cross to our old man. We must reckon that our old man has been crucified and put to an end and that now it is Christ who lives in us. In this way we will contact people not by ourselves but by Christ. This is a matter of practice. To know the doctrine that we have been crucified on the cross and that "it is no longer I who live, but it is Christ who lives in me" (Gal. 2:20) is not sufficient. The urgent need today is that we practice this. If we love the Lord and are seeking His heart, we will realize that the urgent need today is that we practice what we know about Christ in all the affairs of our daily life. The desire of the Lord's heart and what He is seeking for is that we live Him.

We must practice one thing at all times and in all things— to reject our natural life and take Christ as our life. If we practice this, we will realize that each of us is one of the many grains, one member among many members. If we live by our natural life, we will not realize this matter, but if we reject ourselves and take Christ as our life in our daily affairs, we will realize that we are each parts of the Body of Christ and that we need to depend on the other members (Rom. 12:4-5). We may believe that each of us is one grain among many grains, but we may not have this sense or realization in our daily living, because we still live by our natural life. When we practice to give up ourselves and to take Christ as our life, we will realize that we are parts of the increase of Christ.

The Vine and the Branches

The Lord told us not only that we as the many grains are the increase of Christ but also that He is the vine and we are the branches (John 15:5). As branches of this vine, we are the increase of Christ, and just as the branches are the same as the vine in life and in nature, we Christians are the same as Christ in life and in nature.

What is a Christian, and what is the church? A Christian is a part of the church, and the church is the increase of Christ. Thus, we Christians are parts of the increase of Christ. We are branches of the vine and have the life of the vine. We also have another life, the natural life, which causes us to live as something other than branches of the vine and to not sense the need to depend on other Christians. However, if we deny the natural life, take Christ as our life day by day, and live as branches of the vine, we will sense our need for other Christians (1 Cor. 12:19-22). We will realize that we are only members and that we cannot be the increase of Christ by ourselves. It is the entire Body that is the increase of Christ.

The Firstborn among Many Brothers

In John 20 we see that the Lord's brothers are His increase. On the morning of the Lord's resurrection, the Lord appeared to Mary and told her, "Go to My brothers" (v. 17). In 1:14 the Lord is called the only begotten Son of God, but chapter twenty tells us that the Lord has brothers, indicating that the Lord was multiplied. As the only begotten Son of God, He was the one grain. However, through His death and resurrection, He produced the many grains. He, as the original grain, is the first among the many grains, and all the other grains are out of Him. Thus, the only begotten Son of God became the firstborn Son of God (Rom. 8:29) among the many sons who are His increase. The many grains, the branches of the vine, and the many brothers are all the increase of Christ. Christ has been increased; He is no longer merely the one grain or merely the only begotten Son. He has been increased and is now the Firstborn among many brothers.

THE ONENESS OF THE INCREASE OF CHRIST

We must also see the oneness of the increase of Christ. All the grains must be one, all the branches must be one in the one vine, and all the brothers must be one. This is why the Lord prayed in John 17:21-23, "That they all may be one; even as You, Father, are in Me and I in You, that they also may be in Us; that the world may believe that You have sent Me. And the glory which You have given Me I have given to them, that they may be one, even as We are one; I in them, and You in Me, that they may be perfected into one, that the world may know that You have sent Me and have loved them even as You have loved Me."

This passage shows us the basis for our oneness. Verse 21 shows us that Christ is in the Father, the Father is in Christ, and we are one by being in Christ. Verse 22 mentions the glory that the Lord has given to us. This glory is simply the divine life, which the Father gave to the Son and the Son gave to us so that we might be one. We can be one only in the divine life. Verse 23 says, "I in them," indicating that Christ is in us. It is because Christ is in us that we can be perfected into one. Thus, we are in Christ, we have the divine life, and Christ is in us. These are the most important aspects of the basis for our oneness. It is possible for us to be one with others because we are in Christ, we have the divine life, and Christ is in us.

We must realize that we have been put into Christ and are in Christ as our sphere in which we walk, live, and work (1 Cor. 1:30; Col. 2:6). We must remember that day by day we are walking, living, and working in Christ, who is our realm and our everything. In this sphere we are supplied and also limited by Him. The Lord is our pattern; while He was on the earth He always realized that He was in the Father, and He never acted outside of the Father (John 14:10; 5:17, 19). All His activities in His daily life were limited by the Father. Now we are in Him, just as He was in the Father. Thus, we must act, walk, work, and live in Christ, who is our limitation, our sphere, and our everything. When we are outside of Christ, we are outside of the oneness of the Body. When we act apart from Christ, we are detached from the Body of Christ. We must learn the lesson of constantly walking in Christ. This is even related to the matter of the church, which is the increase and counterpart of Christ. We cannot be in the church in actuality apart from Christ. We must walk, live, and work in Christ in order to have the real church life.

Not only are we in Christ, but we also have the same divine life, the one life, which is Christ Himself and also God Himself. We must realize that we have God in Christ as our life, and we must learn to live by this life day by day. This is not a mere doctrine; this is something that is crucial to the church life. If we are going to be the full expression of Christ as the Body of Christ, we must realize that we have the divine life and that we are one in this life. Outside of this life we are many separate individuals, but because we are in this life, we are one.

The final crucial point is that Christ is in us (14:20; 2 Cor 13:5). Without Christ being in us and Christ living in us, we cannot be perfected. An empty cup is imperfect because there is no water within it. Similarly, we are imperfect without Christ living in us. Just as a cup must be filled with water to be perfect, we as vessels of Christ must be filled with Christ in order to be perfected. When we are filled with Christ, we will be one. On the one hand, we will be in Christ as our spiritual realm, and on the other hand, Christ will be in us as our spiritual fullness.

Suppose there is a brother who does everything by himself and within whom Christ has no ground. Such a person will eventually have a sense of emptiness and of being short of something. He will also sense that it is impossible for him to be joined to the other saints. However, one day he may go through a crisis. As a result, he may offer himself to the Lord, take Christ as his life, and truly begin to practice living by Christ. Gradually, day by day, he will be filled with Christ and perfected by Christ. Eventually, he will spontaneously be joined to the other saints.

Our oneness is based on the facts that we are in Christ, that we have the divine life, and that Christ is in us. In our daily living and in all the situations that we encounter, we must take Christ as our life and remember that we are in Christ. If we give the ground in us to Christ so that He may live in us, we will spontaneously have the oneness. We will have Christ as our life, Christ will have the increase among us, and this increase will be realized in the oneness. Through this oneness, the world will know that Christ is the sent One, and Christ will be glorified, magnified, and received by many others (John 17:21, 23). This is the eternal purpose of God.

God is in Christ, and Christ is in us to be our life. If we constantly take Him as our life, apply Him to all the matters in our daily living, and walk, work, and live in Him and let Him live in us to be our perfection, we will be one as the increase of Christ. This will be the testimony of the Body of Christ and the testimony that Christ is the sent One of God. Christ will be glorified and magnified before the world, and as a result, many people will see Him and believe into Him as their Savior. May the Lord be gracious to us that we would practice to apply Christ as our life in our daily living and realize that we are in Christ and that Christ is in us so that we may be one.

CHAPTER THREE

ABIDING IN CHRIST AND LEARNING THE LESSON OF THE CROSS FOR THE ONENESS

Scripture Reading: John 15:5, 8; 17:21-23; Matt. 10:18-20

The Gospel of John reveals Christ as life and the oneness of the Body of Christ. Because of this, it can be considered an extract of the entire Bible, which begins with the tree of life and ends with the holy city (the consummation of the Body of Christ), in which is the tree of life (Gen. 2:9; Rev. 21:2; 22:1-2). These two matters of the tree of life and the holy city are simple yet very mysterious.

MAN BEING CREATED TO CONTAIN CHRIST AS LIFE

The Scriptures reveal that we were created as vessels of God (Rom. 9:21, 23; 2 Tim. 2:20-21). A vessel by itself is empty and must be filled with something. The Scriptures show us that as vessels we must be filled with God (2 Cor. 4:7; Eph. 3:19). God's intention is that we would be containers for Him and that He would fill us with Himself as life. This is why God created man according to His own image, which is Christ Himself (Gen. 1:26; 2 Cor. 4:4; Col. 1:15). The first man, Adam, who was created according to the image of Christ, was a figure or "photograph" of Christ (Rom. 5:14); that is, he had the image of Christ, but he did not have Christ as his life. Thus, God put Adam in front of the tree of life (Gen. 2:8-9) with the intention that he would take of the tree of life and receive Christ as life, but Adam failed to do this. After a long period of time, Christ came to us as life. Christ, who is the expression and embodiment of God, came to present God to us so that we could take Him and gain Him.

We must realize that God's intention is to be life to us and that our relationship with God is a matter of life. According to our natural concept, our relationship with God should be a matter of our doing something for God or worshipping God in a formal way. However, the Scriptures show us something absolutely different. At the very beginning of the Scriptures, God presents Himself to man as the tree of life. Thus, God's intention is that we would take Him as life. When the Lord Jesus came to the earth, instead of demanding that everyone worship Him, He told them that He was the bread of life for them to eat (John 6:35, 48-51). He said, "He who eats Me, he also shall live because of Me" (v. 57). Our relationship with God should be one of taking and enjoying Him as our life.

STOPPING OUR DOING
AND SIMPLY ABIDING IN CHRIST AS THE VINE

God has no intention of asking us to do anything for Him. The concept of doing good and of working for God is from the tree of the knowledge of good and evil, not from the tree of life. Throughout the whole Gospel of John the Lord never told anyone to do anything for Him. Instead, He told us that we need to believe into Him (v. 29). For us to believe into Him is simply to receive Him into us (1:12). The Lord also told us that after receiving Him we must learn how to abide in Him and how to let Him abide in us, just as the branches of a vine abide in the vine and let the vine abide in them. In John 15 the Lord said, "I am the vine; you are the branches. He who abides in Me and I in him, he bears much fruit; for apart from Me you can do nothing....In this is My Father glorified, that you bear much fruit and so you will become My disciples" (vv. 5, 8). The branches of a vine do nothing except abide in the vine and let the vine abide in them. As the branches abide in the vine, the life of the vine in the sap becomes their sufficient supply, and they spontaneously bear fruit. The fruit is not the issue of the branches' good works or doings. Rather, it is the overflow of life, the overflow of the rich sap of the vine.

You must realize that you are a branch of Christ. God has no intention of asking you to do anything for Him, so you should forget about doing good things for God. If you begin to do something for God, He will tell you to stop your doing and simply abide in Christ. Thus, you should simply keep yourself in contact with Christ. Let Christ be everything to you. Let Christ be your life, let Him grow in you, and let Him live Himself out of you. There is nothing for you to do except abide in Christ. What a joy and a rest this is! When many of the Lord's children come to talk to me, they talk only about their negative situations. We must all forget about the negative situations and instead realize the positive situation—that we are branches of Christ and that Christ is our life. If we realized this, we would say, "Hallelujah! I am a branch of Christ, and Christ is in me. He is my life and my everything."

The sisters often tell me that they need more patience in dealing with their children and in handling family matters. They do not realize that Christ is their patience and that as long as they allow Christ to live in them, they will have patience. When we allow Christ to live in us, Christ as patience will prevail, but without Christ living in us, we cannot have patience. The only matter we should focus on is Christ and the glorious fact that we are members of Christ; we should not pay attention to anything else. We are branches of the divine vine, and in this vine Christ is within us and is everything to us. We can apply Him, employ Him, and appropriate Him in such a practical way.

We must realize that we are no longer in Adam. We have been reborn, so we are in Christ and have Christ as life in us. Not only so, we are also parts of Christ as the increase of Christ and parts of the counterpart of Christ. The life, nature, essence, and riches of Christ are within us. May the Lord open our eyes to see that we not only have Christ in us but are also parts of Christ. When we realize this, we will stop doing so many things all the time. We may even stop our old way of praying; instead of praying that the Lord would do various things for us, we may pray that we would abide in Him. The Lord today is living in us. If we abide in Him and let Him abide in us, we will spontaneously be fruit-bearing branches. We do not need to strive to bear fruit, because this is the responsibility of the life within us. We simply need to abide in Christ and enjoy Him.

One day a sister came to me and said, "I understand that Christ is my life and that I have to trust Him regarding my husband. However, I want to know what to do to deal with my husband." Immediately I told this sister that she was outside of Christ. If we must ask what to do regarding a certain matter, we are practically outside of Christ. If we are abiding in Christ, there will be no need for us to ask what to do. Suppose you ask a branch that is abiding in a vine what it is going to do regarding a certain matter. If the branch could speak, it would answer, "I do not know what I am going to do. I only know to abide here and to enjoy the vine. Look how happy and restful I am! I do not have any burdens or even responsibilities. I am simply abiding in the vine and letting the vine abide in me."

Praise the Lord that we are branches of the vine and that Christ is living in us. If we are going to practice abiding in Christ, we need to see the glorious and divine fact that we are vessels, that Christ is our life, and that this life will take care of everything. Christ will live Himself out through us and will be everything to us, including our patience and love. This is the tree of life—the vine with all the branches as its increase bearing fruit all the time. This tree is a picture of the church, which is composed of all the believers. If we would consider this picture of the vine with the branches, we would realize the full, intrinsic significance of what it means to be a Christian and what it means to be the church.

We need a heavenly vision of what we are. We need to see that we are no longer parts of Adam; rather, we are parts of Christ, branches of the divine vine. The life, nature, wealth, and riches of the vine are all in us. Thus, we do not need to do anything; all we need to do is to abide in the vine, to keep ourselves in contact with Christ day by day and moment by moment. This is to keep ourselves in the inner man, which is our spirit, and in contact with the Holy Spirit, who is the reality of Christ (Eph. 3:16; John 14:17).

BECOMING ONE BY BEING BROKEN

In the Gospel of John there is not only the matter of life but also the matter of oneness. After doing so many things on the earth, the Lord prayed to the Father that all the believers would be one in Him. In John 17 He prayed, "That they all may be one; even as You, Father, are in Me and I in You, that they also may be in Us; that the world may believe that You have sent Me. And the glory which You have given Me I have given to them, that they may be one, even as We are one; I in them, and You in Me, that they may be perfected into one, that the world may know that You have sent Me and have loved them even as You have loved Me" (vv. 21-23). The many grains in chapter twelve and the branches in chapter fifteen are equal to the bride as the increase of Christ in chapter three (vv. 29-30). However, the increase of Christ, though it consists of all the believers as the many grains and the many branches, is one, not many (Rom. 12:5). There is only one Body for the Head and only one bride for the Bridegroom. Christ has only one increase, but this one increase consists of all the believers, signified by the many grains and the many branches. Thus, we as individuals are not the increase of Christ but only parts of the increase of Christ.

We as the many grains must become a loaf (1 Cor. 10:17), and the only way we can become a loaf is by being ground and crushed. Otherwise, we cannot be one with others. To produce a loaf of bread, you must grind and crush the grain into flour, mix the flour with water, and bake it. In a similar way, for us as the many grains to be one, we must be broken. Without being broken, there can be no oneness, because in ourselves we are too whole, too perfect. We may be so perfect that we are independent and are unable to be joined with others. Thus, we must be broken. The lesson of brokenness, which is the lesson of the cross, is a serious lesson that we must learn. As perfect, independent saints, we cannot be built up and knit with others. We must be broken so that we would never be perfect in an individual way again. Once a grain is ground and crushed, it can never be perfect again. If we determine to keep our perfection, we will always be independent, and we will never be built up with others as part of the loaf. Thus, we must be broken. This should not be a mere doctrine to us; this should be our practice. We should test ourselves and prove whether we are part of the loaf or still one grain among many grains.

In John 17 the Lord offered a prayer for oneness. The Lord prayed that the Father would do something so that all the grains might be one. He did not pray merely for unity, for the grains to be united, but for oneness, for the grains to be one. In a loaf the grains are not merely united; they become one loaf. This oneness is the Body, the bride, the holy city, and the dwelling place of God. Until this oneness comes into being, there is no way for God to do anything. Today many Christians are praying that they would know the will of God so that they would know what to do in certain situations. However, the will of God cannot be accomplished unless there is this oneness among the saints as the dwelling place of God. We must realize the need for life and oneness. We must stop all our doing and working and instead abide in Christ, keep ourselves in contact with Christ, and learn the lesson of the cross in order to be one with the saints. Then we will have the oneness as the dwelling place of God, and God will be able to accomplish His will.

We must consider these two matters of life and oneness. God's intention is not that we would do anything, because we could never do anything that would be pleasing to God. His intention is that we would take Christ as our life in a practical way. Thus, on the one hand, we need to stop ourselves from trying to do good and always keep ourselves in contact with Christ. On the other hand, we need to learn the lesson of brokenness in order to be one with all the other saints and to be the real expression of Christ as the Body of Christ. Then the Lord will have the ground and the opportunity to do whatever He desires. This is what the Lord is seeking after today.

Chapter Four

BEING MINGLED WITH GOD
TO REALIZE THE ONENESS OF THE BODY

(1)

Scripture Reading: John 3:6; 4:24; Rom. 8:16; 1 Cor. 6:17; John 6:57, 63; 14:20; Gal. 2:20; Matt. 10:19-20; John 17:21-23; 1 Cor. 12:13

There are two crucial matters in the Scriptures—Christ as life and the Body of Christ. We see the first matter at the beginning of the Scriptures, where there is the tree of life, and we see the second matter at the end of the Scriptures, where there is the holy city, a composition of many persons as one Body. This shows us that God's intention is that He would be life to us so that we would be built together in His life as one Body, the holy city. This is the central message of the entire Scriptures.

In this message we would like to see the matters of mingling and oneness. Mingling is related to life, whereas oneness is related to the Body. Mingling is a matter of God becoming life to us (Lev. 2:4-5; 1 Cor. 6:17); when we take God as our life and God becomes life to us, He mingles Himself with us. Oneness, on the other hand, is a matter of the Body. When we saved ones are built together as the Body, we have the oneness. Thus, we may say that God's intention is to become life to us so that we would be built together as one Body. We may also say that God's intention is to mingle Himself with us so that we may become one with Him and with one another.

EATING THE LORD AS OUR SPIRITUAL FOOD
TO BE MINGLED WITH HIM

Many years ago I was taught that our relationship with

God was a matter of union and that we were united with God
and joined to the Lord. However, one day as I was preaching
and teaching this matter of union, the word *mingling* came to
me. I realized that our relationship with God is not only a
matter of union but also a matter of mingling, which is much
deeper. The word *mingled* can be found in Leviticus 2, where
it is used by the Holy Spirit to describe God's desire in His
relationship with man. Verse 5 says that in preparing the meal
offering the oil had to be mingled with the fine flour. The oil
signifies God Himself as the Holy Spirit (Luke 4:18; Heb. 1:9),
and the fine flour signifies the Lord Jesus' humanity. Thus,
the oil being mingled with the fine flour signifies God being
mingled with humanity. The oil and the fine flour signify
divinity and humanity as two different natures being mingled
together as one. However, this mingling does not produce a
third nature; rather, the two natures remain distinguishable
in their combination.

Whatever we eat becomes mingled with us; thus, the best
way for something to become mingled with us is for us to eat it.
Although this is very clear and simple, most of the time we do
not apply this to our relationship with the Lord Jesus. We
must be impressed by the Lord's word in John 6: "I am the
bread of life....He who eats Me, he also shall live because of
Me" (vv. 48, 57). The Lord told us that He is the bread of
life and that we may eat Him. This word concerning eating
the Lord is very simple and practical, yet we do not pay much
attention to it. Have you experienced eating Christ as your
food in order to live by Him? If you have never experienced
Christ in such a practical way, I am concerned for you as
a Christian. We must have some real experiences of Christ.
Every day I have the experience of eating and living by the
food that I eat. If I had not eaten today, I would be tired and
weak. But because I have eaten something, I am refreshed
and strengthened, and I am living by what I ate. Every child
knows how to eat. We must know how to take Christ as our
food, how to eat Him, and how to live by Him. Our taking
the Lord as our food day by day is the only way for God to
be mingled with us. We must all consider and ask ourselves

whether we have had the real experience of taking the Lord as our food day by day and living by Him.

Once I asked a group of believers whether they had had such an experience of taking the Lord as their food and living by Him. One sister told me that she had experienced the Lord in this way many times. She said that whenever she got into trouble or had some burden or difficulty, she would go to the Lord and commit her burdens to Him, and the Lord would take her burdens and bear them Himself. Actually, this is not an experience of taking the Lord as food. Suppose you had a burden, and you asked your food to bear the burden. If your food could speak, it would tell you, "Leave your burden on your shoulders. I want to come into you to be digested by you and energize you to bear the burden. I will not take this burden away from you. Rather, when you eat and digest me, I will become your constituents to energize you to bear the burden. I will be your energy and strength so that you will be able to bear what you by yourself cannot bear."

At a certain time the apostle Paul was given a thorn in his flesh. Because he was just as human as we are, he went to the Lord and prayed three times that the Lord would take the thorn away. However, the Lord said to him, "I will not take the thorn away from you, because My grace is sufficient for you, and My strength is perfected in weakness. My way is not to help you by taking away the thorn. My way is to strengthen you with Myself as the sufficient grace. My grace, which is simply Myself, will be your strength to energize you to suffer the thorn" (2 Cor. 12:7-9). This is the way that the Lord deals with us. Our concept, which is wrong, is that whenever we get into trouble we should go to the Lord and say, "Lord, be merciful to me and remove this trouble." Sometimes the Lord does something to remove the burden or difficulty, but the more we grow in the Lord, the more we will discover that many of the difficulties and troubles that we encounter the Lord does not take away. Instead, the Lord leaves them with us and causes us to learn to take Him as our food and our life supply to become inwardly energized. When our inner man, our spirit, is energized, we become strong enough to bear the burden and suffer all our troubles while praising Him. This is the way the Lord deals with us, and this is the way we can experience the Lord as our food and live by Him. By doing this we will grow with the Lord and in the Lord, and the Lord Himself will increase in us day by day.

THE CHRISTIAN LIFE BEING
THE MINGLING OF GOD WITH MAN

God's eternal purpose is that we would daily take Him as our life, life supply, and food so that He can be mingled with us. All the matters in the Christian life are actually matters of God being mingled with man. For example, what is real Christian love? Real Christian love is the mingling of God with man. When we love others in the Lord, the love with which we love them should be the mingling of God with us. In other words, it should not only be we who are loving them, but it should also be God mingled with us who is loving them. There must be the mingling of God with us in our love. What is Christian patience? Christian patience is nothing but the mingling of God with us. What is real prayer? Real prayer is the mingling of God with us. Andrew Murray once said that real prayer is prayer made by the Christ dwelling in us to the Christ in the heavens. In other words, when we are praying, it should not only be we who are praying but also Christ within us praying. Real prayer is the mingling of Christ with us.

What is real Christian worship? Most Christians think that when we come to worship the Lord, it is best to kneel down, bow our heads, close our eyes, and concentrate our mind on the Lord. However, this is not real Christian worship. Real Christian worship is the mingling of God with us who are Christians. When we come to the Lord's table meeting, we often have the natural concept that we are there to remember the Lord in our mind. Then as we remember Him in our mind, we open our mouths to praise and thank the Lord for how good He is to us and for all the things He has done for us. However, in instituting the Lord's table, the Lord Himself said, "This is My body, which is given for you; this do unto the remembrance of Me....This cup is the new covenant established in My blood; this do, as often as you drink it, unto the remembrance of Me" (1 Cor. 11:24-25). The real remembrance of the Lord is to take Him, drink Him, and feed on Him in our spirit. While we take the bread with our hands, we must enjoy Him in our spirit. The real remembrance of the Lord is to be mingled with the Lord.

Every day and every moment we must practice being mingled with the Lord. Before we begin praying, we must tell Him, "Lord, I am going to pray, but I do not want to pray by myself. While I am praying, I would like You to pray with me and in me." In all the matters and situations that happen to us day by day, we must practice one thing—to live not by ourselves but by the Lord. Even before we begin talking with a brother, we must tell the Lord, "Lord, I am going to talk with this brother, but I do not want to talk with him by myself. While I am speaking with him, I would like You to speak in me." The Lord told us that when we are brought to the rulers and are persecuted, we do not need to consider what to speak or how to speak because the Spirit of the Father will speak in us (Matt. 10:18-20). This is the Christian life. The Christian life is not a life of our living out ourselves but a life of Christ living within us (Gal. 2:20).

In all our daily happenings we must practice taking Christ as our life and living by Him in a practical way. We all know the doctrine of mingling, but now there is a need for the real practice of mingling. Throughout the day we must learn to practice being mingled with the Lord. In order to practice this we must be reminded that the Lord is the Spirit, that we have a spirit, and that we have been reborn in our spirit by the Spirit of the Lord (2 Cor. 3:17; 1 Thes. 5:23; John 3:6). Now the Spirit of the Lord, the Lord Spirit (2 Cor. 3:18b), is living in our spirit. Wherever we go or whatever we do, we must remember that the Lord is now living in our spirit. We must reject and deny our natural life, mind, will, and desires. We must turn to the spirit, the innermost part of our being, to contact the Lord and sense His desire. Then we will sense the Lord's moving and working, and we will know what to say and do. What we do will not be merely out of ourselves. Rather, it will be something done by us yet through the Lord and with the Lord. This is the simple way to take the Lord as our life supply and to live by the Lord. This is something that we must practice all the time.

THE RESULT OF THE MINGLING BEING THE ONENESS

The result of this mingling will be the real oneness among the saints, the oneness of the Body. We have been baptized in the Spirit to be one Body and have been given to drink this one Spirit (1 Cor. 12:13). Thus, the more we drink Him, the more we will be in the one Body. The more we take the Lord as our food and life supply and live by Him, the more we will realize the oneness of the Body. The life by which we live in the Lord is not an individualistic life but a life for the corporate Body and the members of the Body. As those who are in Christ, we are not merely individuals but members of the Body. When we live by the self, we do not feel or sense the need for the Body or the saints. However, when we reject ourselves, deny ourselves, and take the Lord as our life and life supply to live by Him, we sense that we are no longer mere individuals but members of the Body. We sense our need for the other members and realize the oneness of the Body.

The oneness of the Body is a matter of life, not a matter of doctrine, teaching, or organization. As we take Christ as our life and life supply day by day and moment by moment, we will be in the oneness of the Body, because we will be living by the one life. None of us should live by ourselves; rather, we must learn the practical lesson of living by Christ. When we live by Christ, there will be a longing in us to always be related with others and a real desire to be one with all the saints. This oneness is not in doctrine, teaching, or organization but in Christ Himself experienced as our life. If we live in such a way, taking Christ as our life supply moment by moment and applying Christ to all our situations day by day, we will have the inner registration that we can never be separated from the saints, independent of the saints, or individualistic. We will sense that we are simply members of the Body and will treasure the relatedness between us and the other saints. When the oneness is among us, the divine love, the expression of the divine life, will also be among us. We will love one another not in ourselves or by ourselves but in the life of God, which is

Christ Himself. The divine love will be spontaneously expressed among us through our living by Christ. We will be mingled with God and will be in the oneness of the Body.

These are the two most important matters in the Scriptures—being mingled with God and being one with all the saints. As Christians and children of the Lord and as the Body of Christ, the church of God, there must be the mingling and the oneness among us. The mingling is a matter of our relationship with God, and the oneness is a matter of our relatedness with one another. With God we should be mingled, and among the saints we should have the oneness. Both of these matters depend on our practice day by day of denying our natural life, our self, and learning to apply Christ to all the aspects of our daily life. If we practice taking Him as our life supply and living by Him, we will be delivered from the natural life and individualism. May we all be enabled to practice this lesson, that is, to apply Christ to our daily life. Then we will be fully mingled with God and will have the real oneness among us.

CHAPTER FIVE

BEING MINGLED WITH GOD
TO REALIZE THE ONENESS OF THE BODY

(2)

Scripture Reading: John 14:20; 3:26-30; Eph. 2:21-32; 1 Cor. 3:4-12; Rev. 1:12-13, 20; 4:2-3; 21:2-3, 9-12, 14, 18-19, 21, 23; 22:1-2

THE MINGLING OF GOD WITH MAN
AND THE ONENESS OF THE BODY
BEING THE CENTRAL MATTER IN THE BIBLE
AND IN OUR CHRISTIAN LIFE

In this message we will continue to fellowship about the mingling and the oneness. The mingling is related to life, and the oneness is related to the Body. If we thoroughly study the Scriptures, we will see that these two matters—life and the Body, or the mingling and the oneness—are two central matters in the Scriptures. God's eternal purpose is that He would be life to us and as our life be mingled with us. Thus, the matter of life involves the mingling of divinity with humanity, and the result of this mingling is the Body, the oneness.

There are two pictures in the Scriptures. The first picture, which is in Genesis 2, is a picture of life, and the central item in this picture is the tree of life (v. 9). At the end of the Scriptures is another picture portraying a holy city (Rev. 21:2—22:5). A city is a single entity composed of many pieces of material. Thus, this city is a picture of the oneness. Within this city is the tree of life (22:2), showing us that the oneness is the issue of life. This city comes into being through the flowing of life. The first picture in the Scriptures contains a tree of life and a flowing river, issuing in the material for the building—gold, bdellium, and onyx, which is a precious stone (Gen. 2:9-12). In the first picture there is only the life with the material; there is no building yet. In the second picture, however, the material has been built together into a building, the holy city, New Jerusalem, which is built with gold, pearl, and precious stones (Rev. 21:18-21). If we study these two pictures carefully, we will realize that God's desire is to build a city by the growth of His divine life in many believers. In other words, His desire is for life and building, for mingling and oneness.

What the Lord has been doing and is still doing throughout the generations is building up a city, a Body, by His divine life. This thought runs throughout the entire Bible. The ministry of the apostle Paul, who represents all the gifted ones, is very much concerned with these two matters of life and building. On the one hand, he tells us that Christ is life to us and that we have to take Christ as our life and live by Christ (Col. 3:4). He even says that to live is Christ (Phil. 1:21a). On the other hand, Paul says many things about the building. As those who enjoy Christ as life, we should be built together as the habitation of God (Eph. 2:21-22). Thus, in the ministry of the apostle Paul there are these two central matters—life and the Body, that is, the mingling of God with man and the oneness of the Body.

We need to spend some time to consider what is most important to us as Christians. If we would spend a little time with the Lord to do this, I believe that the Holy Spirit would show us that there are only two matters that are important and vital to us as Christians. One matter is that of taking Christ and experiencing Him as life day by day and moment by moment, even to the extent that we could say with Paul, "To me, to live is Christ" (Phil. 1:21a). Christians like to talk about spirituality and being spiritual. However, what is spirituality, and what does it mean to be spiritual? To be spiritual is simply to live Christ. Genuine spirituality is nothing less than Christ being lived out by us. It is our taking Christ as our life and experiencing Him in a very practical way. Christ as our life must be everything to us in our Christian life; whatever we do must be Christ lived out by us.

The result of such a Christian life is the second important matter—the building together of the saints. Spiritual building is produced only by spiritual growth. The apostle Paul tells us that we are God's farm and God's building (1 Cor. 3:9). The farm implies our growth, and the building implies our being built together. The way to be built together is simply by growing. If we do not grow in the life of Christ, we can never be built together with others. We are built together only by growing in Christ as our life. If I live by my own life and another brother lives by his own life, we will never be built together. Instead of being built together we will quarrel or even fight with each other. This is the same for husbands and wives. I do not believe that there has been one couple who have been married for several years without quarreling. There is only one way that we can be joined, blended, and built together— by the growth of the divine life. Each of us is so peculiar that we would never get along if the Lord were not our life. If an American brother lives by his American culture and a Chinese brother lives by his Chinese culture, they will frequently have problems with each other. We can never work together or be blended as one in this way. However, praise the Lord for the divine "cement," the divine life, which holds us together! We are like stones; when we are by ourselves, we are separate, but when we are put into the divine "cement," which is the divine life, we are cemented together as one, and nothing is able to break us. Oneness is the issue of the mingling of the life of God with us.

THE WAY TO HAVE THE MINGLING AND THE ONENESS

We may realize the importance of these two matters—the mingling of the divine life with man and the oneness of the Body—but now we must ask ourselves how much we have been mingled with the divine life and how much we are actually in the oneness of the Body. Do we have the mingling and the oneness in our Christian life? We should forget about all other things and spend some time before the Lord to consider ourselves with respect to these two matters. The extent to which the Lord values us depends on how much of the divine mingling we have and how much we are in the oneness of the Body.

These two matters are not merely a wonderful teaching or something that will take place in the heavens or in eternity. The way to realize and practice these two matters is simple and practical. Second Corinthians 3:17 tells us that today the Lord is the Spirit. The Bible also tells us that we have been reborn in our spirit (John 3:6) and that our spirit has been renewed through regeneration (Ezek. 36:26; Rom. 7:6). Furthermore, the Lord Spirit is living within our spirit, and these two spirits—the Lord Spirit and our spirit—have been joined and mingled together as one spirit (Rom. 8:16; 1 Cor. 6:17). There are at least three verses in the Scriptures that mention both the divine Spirit and our human spirit. John 3:6 says, "That which is born of the Spirit is spirit," John 4:24 says, "God is Spirit, and those who worship Him must worship in spirit," and Romans 8:16 says, "The Spirit Himself witnesses with our spirit." These verses reveal that the Spirit of the Lord and our spirit have been joined together and work together.

Today the Lord is one with us, and we are one with Him. However, it is not in our mind or our mentality that we are one with Him. Rather, we are one with Him in our spirit, the innermost part of our being. It is a divine and spiritual mystery that the Lord Spirit has mingled Himself with our spirit as one spirit. Thus, the way to take the Lord as our life is not by thinking or using our mind but by exercising our spirit to contact the Lord as the Spirit.

This is not something that we do once for all. Rather, we need to contact the Lord moment by moment. We can never graduate from the things of life. In the realm of knowledge there is a day in which we may graduate from a field of study. We may say, "I have been studying this subject for eight years, and now I will graduate." However, we cannot say, "I have been eating for eighteen years, and now I will graduate from eating." We can never graduate from eating; to graduate from eating is to die. Even more, we cannot graduate from breathing. Similarly, we cannot graduate from contacting the Lord. We must keep ourselves in contact with the Lord all the time.

For example, consider an electric lamp. The lamp may be connected to the electricity, but in order for the lamp to shine, we must turn the switch on. Whenever we turn the switch off, the lamp stops shining. I am afraid that in our Christian life the "switch" has been turned off for quite a long time. We may not even know that there is a switch, much less know how to turn the switch on. Perhaps on occasion we blindly turned the switch on without knowing how we did it. Actually, the way to turn the switch on is very simple. All we need to do is simply contact the Lord by exercising our spirit.

Once a brother told me, "I have been praying for God to give me a big spiritual battery that would be sufficient for a certain amount of time." I said, "Brother, your prayer will never be answered. The Lord cannot give you a spiritual battery. The Lord can only be like an electrical current that is flowing all the time. If you stay in contact with the Lord, you will sense the flow of the current. However, if you turn off the switch, the current will stop, and you will suffer spiritual death. You will stop experiencing all the riches that are in Christ. You must exercise to learn how to turn the switch on and how to keep the switch on."

What is the real Christian life? The real Christian life is Christ being lived out through us. We have our own personality and our own human life, but we should not live by this human life. Instead, we should turn to the divine life, which is Christ Himself living within our spirit. We must do this not once in a while or even once a day but all the time and in every situation. We must deny our natural human life and turn to Christ, exercising our spirit to contact this living person. The religion of Christianity cannot save or deliver us, nor can mere Christian teachings. Only Christ Himself, who is the living Lord and a living person, is able to deliver us. Today we are contacting a living person—Christ Himself. Day by day and moment by moment we should realize that Christ is life in our spirit. He is so real and living, and He is moving and working in us. When we turn to Him in our spirit, He motivates us to live, energizes us to walk, and strengthens us to work. Then it is no longer we who live but He and we living together (Gal. 2:20).

This mingling of the divine life with the human life is the real Christian life. In our love toward others there should be such a mingling. In our service in the church there should be such a mingling. We should be able to say with assurance, "Lord, although I am serving You, You are actually serving within me. Although I am praying to You, You are actually praying within me. I am not doing these things merely by myself. Rather, You are strengthening me within to do everything." What a wonder, a miracle, a rest, and a joy this is! There is no need for us to try to do anything. We should not try by ourselves to overcome sin, to be patient, or to do good things. Instead, we must see that today we have the glorious Christ within us as our life. Simply pay attention to this fact and say, "Hallelujah, praise the Lord! Lord, You are my life within. I can take You as my life and experience You in the way of life. I can take You and experience You not just once a day or in certain matters but day by day, all the time, and in all my circumstances." If we experience Christ in such a way, we will be in the heavenlies, all the sinful and worldly things would be under our feet, and we would be spiritually enriched.

Whenever we are going to do something, we must do it by letting the Lord do it through us. We must even worship God by letting the Lord worship through us (see Hebrews 2:12 and note 3 in the Recovery Version). We can worship God in one of two ways—in an objective way or in a subjective way. Do we worship an objective God or a subjective God? The fact is that today most Christians worship the Lord in an objective way. However, we must realize that the Lord whom we worship is the One who is living within us. While we worship and seek Him, He strengthens us in our spirit to worship Him and energizes us to praise and thank Him. This is real peace and rest. As Christians we should worship the God who is in us and who has mingled Himself with us. This is the simple and practical way to realize the mingling of God with man.

THE NEW JERUSALEM BEING
A COMPOSITION OF ALL THE BELIEVERS

Now we must say something regarding the oneness as seen

in the New Jerusalem. First, we must realize that the holy city, New Jerusalem, is not a place but a person, the bride of the Lamb. The apostle John clearly tells us this in Revelation 21:2. The bride cannot be a place; no one would marry a physical place as his wife. Rather, the bride is a composition of all the redeemed ones of God. In the Gospel of John, John the Baptist said, "He who has the bride is the bridegroom" (3:29a). He mentioned this after his disciples came to him and told him that all the people were following the Lord Jesus. In response, John told his disciples that he was not the Christ and that it was the Lord Jesus who was the bridegroom and who should have the bride. This indicates that the bride is a composition of people. The bridegroom is Christ Himself, and the bride whom He will have is a composition of all the believers. Thus, the holy city, New Jerusalem, is a composition of all the believers.

Revelation also tells us that on the twelve gates of the New Jerusalem are the twelve names of the twelve tribes of Israel (21:12). The twelve tribes represent the redeemed ones in the Old Testament. Furthermore, the twelve foundations of the New Jerusalem bear the names of the twelve apostles, representing all the saved ones in the New Testament age (v. 14). Thus, it is quite clear that the holy city is a composition of all the saved ones throughout the generations.

This corresponds with the apostle Paul's thought and teaching. In the book of Ephesians, Paul indicates that the church is, on the one hand, the wife of Christ and, on the other hand, the habitation of God and that we are like stones that are being built together into the habitation of God (5:31-32; 2:20-22). This is the same as the New Jerusalem— on the one hand, it is the bride of the Lamb, but on the other hand, it is the tabernacle, which is the habitation of God (Rev. 21:2-3). We as the precious stones are being built together as the holy city. Paul also tells us that the church is built with gold, silver, and precious stones (1 Cor. 3:9-12), and at the end of the Scriptures we are told that the holy city is built with similar materials (Rev. 21:18-21).

We should be renewed from our concept of the New Jerusalem as a physical, heavenly building. The New Jerusalem is a composition of living persons to be the living bride of Christ and the living habitation of God. The holy city is a building in which all the saved ones are built together as one Body. How does this building come into being? It comes into being through the mingling of God with man. The believers are the stones, or materials, of this building, and God is within them. From the throne of God flows a river of living water, and along this river grows the tree of life, whose fruit is the life supply to all those who belong to this city (22:1-2). This picture clearly shows us that God as life and the life supply is being mingled with all the saved ones to produce the holy city. Thus, we can see the mingling and the oneness of the Body in this picture.

This picture as the conclusion of the entire Bible reveals to us that God as life and the life supply wants to be mingled with us in order to produce the Body. This Body, which ultimately is the holy city, is the corporate expression of God. God is the content of the city, and the city is the expression of God, having the appearance of God. In Revelation 4 we are told that the appearance of God on the throne is like jasper (vv. 2-3). Later, Revelation tells us that the appearance of the whole city is like jasper and that the wall of the city is built with jasper stone (21:11, 18). Even the first and top foundation of the wall is jasper (v. 19). This shows us that the appearance of the holy city is the appearance of God Himself. In other words, the city is the expression of God.

In the Gospel of John we are told that the Lord came to give us life (10:10), and toward the end of the book the Lord prayed that all those who have His life would be one (17:21-22). In Revelation we see the fulfillment of this prayer in all the saints who are built together as lampstands in each locality (1:11-12). The saints are no longer merely individuals; they are one as lampstands in each locality. Revelation mainly shows us not the individual Christian but a corporate life, a corporate Body. At the beginning of Revelation there are the lampstands, and at the end there is a holy city, in which God as the light is in the Lamb as the lamp (21:23). God is the light, the Lamb is the lamp, and the holy city is the lampstand built of gold (v. 18), like the golden lampstands in Revelation 1.

Thus, the lampstands in Revelation 1 are miniatures of the holy city in Revelation 21.

If we take Christ as our life and live Christ, we will be built up together as one. In other words, our oneness is not an issue of our being organized together but of our growing together. We all need to live by Christ. When we are all living by Christ, we will grow up into one in Christ (Eph. 4:15-16). We will constantly be growing and will be built together as one. The oneness is like a thermometer—it can tell us how much we are in the mingling. If there is no oneness, this proves that there is a lack of mingling. If we are being mingled with God, there will be the oneness of the Body. This is the desire of the Lord's heart. The Lord is seeking after these two matters—the mingling of life and the oneness of the Body, which are Christ and the church. We need to pray for this and look to Him for the grace that we need to practice taking Christ as our life. Then we will be one, and there will be a real oneness among us. We will be full of life, and we will be the real expression of Christ. This is the golden lampstand today and ultimately the holy city in eternity.

CHAPTER SIX

THE NEED FOR A LOVING HEART
AND A RECEIVING SPIRIT TO EAT THE LORD

Scripture Reading: Matt. 5:8; Psa. 73:1; Matt. 15:8; Psa. 51:10;
1 Cor. 2:16; Phil. 2:5; 2 Cor. 3:15-18; Eph. 3:16-17, 19b; 2 Cor.
13:14

Mingling is a very basic concept in the Scriptures. God's
ultimate intention is to be life and everything to us so that
He may mingle Himself with us. At the time of creation man
was made according to the image of God but did not have the
life of God (Gen. 1:26). We were made as vessels of God so that
He could be our content, our life, and our everything (Rom.
9:21, 23). We must realize that we are merely containers and
that the Lord Himself must be our content. Thus, immediately after man was created, God offered Himself to man in
the form of the tree of life (Gen. 2:9). God did not ask,
demand, or command man to do anything. Instead, He only
intended that man would take Him as his life.

EATING VERSUS DOING

Today there is a concept within us that is absolutely con-
trary to the thought of God. Whenever we think about God,
we have the concept that we must do something for Him. We
think that we have to worship Him, fear Him, do His will, and
do good things to please Him. However, the basic thought of
God in the Scriptures is that we would take God as our life in
the same way that we take food. After God created man, He
immediately brought up the matter of eating. At that time
God did not tell Adam to do many different things; instead,
He advised Adam to take care of his eating (vv. 16-17). God
told Adam that he had to eat the proper thing. Our concept is

not one of eating but of doing. We are "doing" and "working" Christians. The Lord's intention, though, is that we would be "eating" Christians. We should be those who eat and drink, not those who merely do things and work. If we eat properly, we will be the proper people. If we do not eat properly, we will not be the right people and will be unable to do what is right. We must realize that God's intention is that we would take Him as food. In other words, we must eat and drink of Christ as our spiritual food and drink (John 6:57; 4:10, 14; 7:37-38). If we feed on Christ and drink of Him, He will be everything to us, and we will be the proper people.

Thus, we must first pay attention to the matters of eating and drinking, not the matters of doing and working. If someone came to the Lord, asking, "What shall I do?" the Lord might answer, "You must eat Me and drink Me. I am like a piece of bread; I am the bread of life. He who eats Me shall live because of Me" (John 6:35, 57). It is not a question of what we should do but a question of what we should eat and by what we should live. It is not a matter of doing and working but a matter of eating and living. We must eat the Lord in order to live by Him. When we take the Lord as our food, He can live through us. May we all have a change in our concept.

One time after I had given several messages on this subject, a brother came to me, saying, "Brother Lee, the messages have been wonderful, but now that we know that we have to do the Lord's will, what should we do?" I clearly told him that it is not a matter of doing or working but a matter of eating, drinking, and living. Our responsibility is to eat Christ, drink Christ, and live Christ. The Bible tells us that the Lord is the bread of life and that he who eats Him will live because of Him (John 6:48, 57). Thus, we must eat the Lord and feed on Him. We are also told that the Lord is the living water, the water of life (4:10). Thus, we must also come to Him and drink Him. Furthermore, the Lord is our life, and it is no longer we who live but the Lord Himself who lives within us (Gal. 2:20). We need to live in the Lord, by the Lord, and for the Lord. May we all have a real change in our concept. We must forget about our doing and working and instead deal with our eating, drinking, and living.

Once a sister came to me, saying, "Brother Lee, I know that as a sister, a wife should submit to her husband, but to tell you the truth, I simply cannot submit to my husband. Can you tell me what I should do? I feel so helpless." I said, "It is good to feel helpless. The more helpless you are, the more you are unable to do anything. Those who are helpless and dead cannot do anything. You must forget about doing anything." She said, "But what should I do when I go back home?" Again, she was raising up the matter of doing. After some consideration, I said, "Let us kneel down and pray together, and when you go back home, the first thing you must do is kneel down to contact the Lord." She said, "Brother Lee, I cannot kneel down and pray to the Lord, because I know that He wants me to submit to my husband, but I do not want to. How can I go to the Lord and pray to Him?" I said, "Just go to the Lord and tell Him what you have told me. Tell Him, 'Lord, I know that You want me to submit to my husband, but I do not want to.'" As soon as this sister contacted the Lord, there was a willingness within her to submit to her husband. This was not her doing; this was the issue of her eating. She contacted the Lord and was strengthened by Him and satisfied with Him. Because she ate the Lord, she received a little more mingling with the Lord and was able to live by Him. This is the basic thought of the whole Scriptures. We all must learn to practice eating and drinking the Lord. Only by eating and drinking the Lord can we take the Lord into our being. If we go to the Lord, contact Him, feed on Him, and drink Him, wonderful things will happen as an issue of our eating and drinking Him.

THE NEED FOR A LOVING HEART
AND A RECEIVING SPIRIT

The Bible reveals that we were made as vessels so that the Lord could be our life and content. It is rather easy to take a cup and to fill it with water. It is not so easy, though, for God to fill us with Himself. In order to be filled, we need a heart that loves the Lord and a spirit to receive the Lord. Thus, when we were regenerated, the Lord renewed our heart and our spirit. Ezekiel 36:26-27 says that the Lord gave us a new heart and a new spirit and that He put His own Spirit into us.

As physical beings, we need food. However, in order to receive the food, we need a heart to desire the food and a mouth and stomach to receive the food. Without a heart to desire the food and a mouth and stomach to receive the food, we could never take in the food. Sometimes we cannot eat because we do not have the appetite, and other times we cannot eat because there is a problem with our mouth or an ulcer in our stomach. Thus, even though the food may be quite delicious, and though we may truly need it, we may be unable to eat it. This is often the situation in our relationship with God. Many times we simply do not have a heart for Him. Even though we may pray to Him with our mouth, our heart may be far away from Him (Matt. 15:8). Furthermore, we may not know how to exercise our spirit to receive Him. How can we receive the Lord if our heart is far from Him and we do not know how to use our spirit?

The real Christian life is not a matter of teaching; it is a matter of Christ Himself as a living person. It is not good enough to come to the Lord merely to learn something. We must come to contact the Lord as a living person and take Him as our food. When we come to a meal, there is no need to learn anything. What we need is an appetite and to know how to exercise our mouth and our stomach to take in the food. Whenever we come to a meeting, to the Word, or to the Lord directly, we must exercise our heart to love Him and exercise our spirit to contact, take in, and receive Him. However, many times when we come to the meetings or read the Word, we do not have a heart that is turned toward the Lord, or we do not know how to exercise our spirit to contact the Lord. We are like people who are sitting at a dining table spread with delicious food but are only looking at and examining the food, not knowing how to exercise our mouths and stomachs to eat the food. We must ask ourselves whether or not we have a real, sincere heart that loves the Lord and whether or not we know the best way to exercise our spirit to contact the Lord. We may have a brilliant mind, but do we have a loving heart and a seeking spirit? Do we have a sincere heart and a right spirit toward the Lord? Our primary responsibility is not to learn about the Lord but to take and receive the Lord. We must take the Lord in first by our heart and then by our spirit. We must exercise our heart to love the Lord and exercise our spirit to take in, contact, and receive the Lord. This is not a doctrine; this is a spiritual reality.

The Lord is so real and living to us because He is the Spirit and is in our spirit. If we know how to exercise our spirit, we will be able to contact the Lord and be in the current of the transmitting Spirit. The Holy Spirit as the transmitting current will transmit the essence of the Lord into us. However, we must allow our concepts and thoughts to be adjusted and corrected. It is not by thinking in our mind that we contact the Lord; rather, it is by loving the Lord with our heart and receiving Him with our spirit. We must pray again and again that the Lord would enable us to love Him. Day and night, morning and evening, we must pray that the Lord would strengthen us to love Him in a full way. The more we love the Lord, the more our heart will be purified and renewed.

DEALING WITH THE HEART

In order to have a heart that loves the Lord, we must deal with our heart, which has four parts—the conscience, the mind, the will, and the emotion (Heb. 10:22; Matt. 9:4; Heb. 4:12; John 16:6, 22). The conscience must be purified and cleansed by the precious blood of Jesus. We must have a conscience without offense (Acts 24:16). If there is any condemnation or offense in our conscience, this will spoil our heart, and our heart will not be at peace. Thus, we must confess all our sins to the Lord and have our conscience sprinkled from every evil thing. Then we will have a conscience void of offense and will be at peace in our heart.

Furthermore, our mind must be simplified. When we are with the Lord, we should not consider or think too much. Instead, we should be simple in our mind. We must be careful that our thoughts would not be corrupted by the enemy from the simplicity toward Christ (2 Cor. 11:3). The brothers must especially be careful not to exercise their mind too much. If you have a brilliant mind and exercise it too much, your mind may be corrupted from the simplicity toward the Lord by too much considering. Much of the time we are troubled by this kind of corruption. Therefore, we must ask the Lord to simplify our mind. We must have a mind like a child's (Matt. 18:3; Mark 10:15). Also, our will must be meek and soft, and our emotion must be full of love. Then our heart will be a right heart, a pure heart, and a heart that loves the Lord. This was the kind of heart that Mary had as she poured the precious ointment upon the Lord (Matt. 26:7). Her heart was a heart with a clean conscience, a simple mind, a meek will, and an emotion full of love. How she loved the Lord! We must ask the Lord to give us such a heart and to renew our heart to such a condition.

EXPERIENCING THE MINGLING BY EATING

When we have such a pure heart, we will have the presence of the Lord. "Blessed are the pure in heart, for they shall see God" (Matt. 5:8). Having a pure heart will enable us to be in the presence of God and to see God. However, being in the presence of God and seeing God are one thing; taking God in is another thing. It is one thing to be at a table in the presence of food, and it is another thing to actually take in the food. Today many Christians talk about the presence of God in the Old Testament sense, but the New Testament shows us something deeper. The New Testament shows us that the Lord Himself lives within us and that for us to live is Christ (Gal. 2:20; Phil. 1:21). Not only is the presence of the Lord with us, but the Lord Himself lives within us and is even mingled with us. If you merely had the presence of a piece of bread, would you be satisfied? No, you would tell the bread, "This is not good enough for me. I must take you in and digest you in order for you to be the very element of my being. Your presence being with me is not good enough. I must take you in and digest you in order for you to become my element." This is the New Testament blessing. Many of us are still used to praying, "Lord, grant us Your presence." I have done this as well, but after praying in such a way, I would tell myself, "What is this? You do not merely have the presence of the

Lord. The Lord today is food to you. You can take, eat, and digest Him, and He can be mingled with you, become a part of you, and become the very element of your being." How wonderful this is! This is the mingling of God with man. Just as tea is mingled with water, the Lord today is mingled with us in our spirit. The Lord is being mingled with us as our life and content, and we are the vessels as His containers.

There needs to be a change in our thinking. We must realize that we were not meant to do anything for Him; we were meant to enjoy Him and apply Him. We must remember that we are nothing but containers of the Lord and that the Lord should be our content. Our mind is a container for the Lord's mind, and the Lord's mind should be the content of our mind (Phil. 2:5). The same is true of our will and emotion; our will is simply a container that must be filled by the will of the Lord, and our emotion is a container that must be filled with the emotions and love of the Lord (Acts 16:7; Phil. 1:8). Every part of our being is a container. Just as our spirit is a container, our mind, will, and emotion are also containers. We must let the Lord fill us and occupy us in every part of our being (Eph. 3:17). We must let Him fill our mind, will, and emotion. Then we will have the mind of Christ, the will of the Lord, and the love and emotion of the Lord, as well as having the Spirit of the Lord in our spirit. Our whole being will be saturated by and with the Lord.

If we want to be in the divine mingling, we must forget about our doing and working. Instead, we must pay our full attention to the matters of eating and drinking. Day by day we should be eating and drinking Christians, not doing and working Christians. For example, when we come to the meeting and sit down, we often consider what we should do in the meeting. However, we should not think about what to do. Rather, we should contact the Lord, feed on the Lord, and drink Him. We should give up the thought of doing something and simply contact Him. We should say, "Lord, thank You that once again I have the opportunity to contact You." Some people enjoy having a cup of coffee for refreshment. In a similar way, we should remind ourselves to take "a cup of Christ." We should always take the chance to take in the Lord. When we are going to visit a brother, we should not consider what to say or what to do. We should simply contact the Lord, feed on the Lord, and drink the Lord, and then something will flow out as living water as the issue of our contact with the Lord, not of our doing or working.

Even when we are ministering the word, we must forget about what we are doing and simply keep ourselves in contact with the Lord. While we are ministering, we should be feeding on the Lord and drinking the Lord. For example, while a lamp is shining, it is simultaneously being supplied. If a lamp could speak, it would tell you, "I do not know how to shine; I only know how to enjoy the supply. The shining is simply an issue of the supply. I do not have to worry about the shining; I simply abide in the electrical current and enjoy it." We must forget about our doing and working and instead learn how to enjoy the Lord, eat the Lord, and drink the Lord. This is not a doctrine but a spiritual reality. We must learn how to love Him with our heart and enjoy Him with our spirit. The Lord has given us a new heart and a new spirit and has put His Spirit into our spirit that we may enjoy Him all the time. We must ask the Lord to create a new heart in us, a heart that is clean and pure, and to give us a right spirit that we may exercise our spirit to contact Him (Psa. 51:10). By doing this we will constantly be filled with the Lord and occupied by the Lord. Then our whole being will be transformed into the image of the Lord, the Lord will be formed in us, and we will be conformed to the image of the Lord (2 Cor. 3:18; Gal. 4:19; Rom. 8:29).

CHAPTER SEVEN

EATING THE LORD
BY PRAYING OVER THE WORD

Scripture Reading: Psa. 36:7-9; 34:8; 42:1-2; Matt. 4:4; 1 Pet. 2:2-3; 1 Cor. 10:3-4; 12:13; John 6:57, 63

EATING AND DRINKING CHRIST

God's eternal intention, which is the central thought of the Bible, is that we would be mingled with God and become the Body of Christ by eating, drinking, and even digesting Him as our spiritual food. This matter of eating is revealed at the beginning of the Scriptures. It was the first matter that God raised up with man after creating man (Gen. 2:16-17). God told man that he had to eat the proper thing, and if we examine the Scriptures carefully, we will realize that the proper thing for man to eat and to take as his food supply is God Himself. Man was created as a vessel to contain God (Rom. 9:21, 23). Thus, we must take God into us as our content. God has revealed that the way for us to take Him in is by eating and drinking Him. In the Gospel of John the Lord Himself said, "I am the bread of life," and "He who eats Me, he also shall live because of Me" (6:48, 57). Many Christians are concerned with knowing about the Lord, but not many have seen that the Scriptures reveal that we must also eat and drink the Lord. In the Old Testament the psalmist said, "As the hart pants / After the streams of water, / So my soul pants / For You, O God / My soul thirsts for God, / For the living God" (Psa. 42:1-2a). The psalmist was thirsty for God as the living water (cf. John 4:10). In the New Testament the apostle Paul tells us that the manna and the water that the people of Israel ate and drank in the wilderness are both types of Christ (1 Cor.

10:3-4). Today, since we have Christ as the reality of the types, we must make eating and drinking the Lord our reality. First Corinthians 12:13 tells us that we have not only been baptized in the Spirit but have also been made to drink of this Spirit. We must eat and drink the Lord as the Spirit.

We must be deeply impressed regarding our need to eat and drink the Lord. The experience of eating and drinking a certain thing is much more subjective than merely knowing about it. We may know many things about bread and milk, but if we do not eat and drink the bread and milk, they will remain objective and be of no value to us. The most important thing is that we take the bread and milk into us by eating and drinking them. Similarly, we may know many teachings about Christ, but if we do not eat and drink Christ, Christ will remain objective to us. This does not mean that Christian teachings are bad; they are actually good and necessary, but this depends on what we do with them. We must certainly know about the person and work of Christ, but the main thing is that we receive Him in a practical and subjective way by eating and drinking Him.

In order to take Christ as our food and drink, we must be very simple. One does not need a great amount of knowledge in order to eat. In fact, our knowledge often complicates us and hinders us from eating Christ. After I was regenerated, I was taught many Christian teachings and was trained in a profound way. Consequently, I became a complicated person. However, today I am a very simple Christian. Being a Christian is less a matter of knowing and more a matter of eating and drinking Christ day by day and moment by moment. We need to be simple and take in the Lord as our food and drink.

PRAYING OVER THE WORD

We must realize that the Lord today is the Spirit (2 Cor. 3:17) and that the Lord is also the Word (John 1:1, 14). These are the two biggest gifts we have as Christians—the Spirit within our spirit and the Word of God in our hands (Rom. 8:16; 2 Tim. 3:16). Thus, if we want to eat and drink Christ, we must come to the Word of God and enjoy the Spirit.

In order to receive the Lord through the Word, we must

exercise our spirit. If we want to look at something, we will automatically exercise our eyes. If we want to hear something, we will spontaneously use our ears. If we are going to walk or run, we will begin to exercise our legs and feet. Similarly, when we are going to pray, we must exercise our spirit (Eph. 6:17-18). Without exercising our spirit, we cannot pray in a proper way. Since we may be accustomed to praying from our mind, we need to practice exercising our spirit. When a baby first begins to move around, he mainly uses his hands and arms. However, as he continues to move around, he eventually reaches a point at which he begins to use his feet and legs. Likewise, when we begin praying, we often begin by using our mind, but after praying continually for a while, we will reach a point at which we will begin to exercise our spirit.

We must pray over what we read in the Word and take in what we read by exercising our spirit. Ephesians 6:17 and 18 tell us to "receive the helmet of salvation and the sword of the Spirit, which Spirit is the word of God, by means of all prayer and petition, praying at every time in spirit and watching unto this in all perseverance and petition concerning all the saints." We should receive the word of God not merely by exercising our mind to understand but by means of all prayer and petition, praying by exercising our spirit. By this, the word becomes spirit and life to us in our experience (John 6:63). For instance, Philippians 2:6 says, "Who, existing in the form of God, did not consider being equal with God a treasure to be grasped." In taking this verse, we may pray, "Lord, You have the form of God. I praise and worship You that You have the form of God." Just as we eat bread by taking a little piece and chewing it, we should simply take a short phrase of a verse and turn the words of the Bible into our prayer. Then we may take the next phrase and "chew" on it by praying. When we pray over the Word in such a way, we eat and drink the Lord who is the Word of God. This kind of practice is vital to our Christian life. This practice will cause the Word to become the life supply to our spirit instead of mere knowledge to our mind. There are all kinds of food and riches stored in the Bible, and our urgent need is to take and receive them little by little.

If we read through the Bible in this way, we will be fed and filled. As the psalmist said, we will be saturated with the fatness of the Lord's house and drink of the river of His pleasures (Psa. 36:8). If we exercise our spirit to pray over the Word, we will be satisfied, strengthened, and refreshed. However, if we merely take the Word in as knowledge, we will become proud. We will think that we have spiritual vision or revelation, when in fact we may not. Knowledge makes us proud (1 Cor. 8:1), but the inward working of the Spirit makes us humble. If we take the Word as our life supply, as the Lord Himself, we will spontaneously be humble, because the Lord as the humble One will live in us. Also, if we do this, our spirit will be strong, living, and active in the meetings and in our daily life. Many Christians are weak in their spirit because they exercise their mind too much to merely study the Word and do not spend enough time exercising their spirit to pray. Thus, although they may be experts in the doctrinal knowledge of the Bible, it is difficult for them to pray. The more we take the Word in by praying over it, the more our spirit will be strengthened. I have diligently studied the Scriptures for many years, and today I continue to study them. However, my way of studying is different than it was before. When I was young, I studied merely with my mind, but today I do not merely study the Word with my mind but also take the Word into my being by praying over the Word.

Many things may begin to happen when we pray over the Word. The Lord will speak to us from the Word, using the words that we read to converse with us. For instance, we may read Philippians 2:7, which says that the Lord "emptied Himself, taking the form of a slave, becoming in the likeness of men." We may tell the Lord, "Lord, thank You for emptying Yourself," but then the Lord may ask us, "What about you? Have you emptied yourself?" Then we may repent to the Lord for not emptying ourselves. Furthermore, the Lord may check with us regarding our spouse or the saints, which may lead us to intercede for them. Thus, the Lord will use the words that we read to converse with us. In this way the Lord will adjust us, correct us, enlighten us, cleanse us, and anoint us.

If our time is occupied with this kind of prayer, and it

turns out that there is no time left to pray for our situations, we may tell the Lord, "Lord, there are many matters on my heart, and there is no time to pray for them. You know what is in my heart; take care of all these matters." The Word promises that if we seek first the kingdom and His righteousness, all our daily needs will be added to us (Matt. 6:33).

ABIDING IN THE LORD
BY STAYING IN CONTACT WITH HIM

If we practice praying over the Word, we will experience the Lord in a very living way, and after a period of time we will be accustomed to speaking to the Lord in a very living yet ordinary and conversational way. We will speak with the Lord not only when we are by ourselves in a private room but also while we are talking with others. We will be constantly in contact with the Lord. Our prayer will be spontaneous and automatic, as natural to us as breathing (1 Thes. 5:17).

Many of us may have been Christians for a long time, yet we still are not accustomed to contacting the Lord. We may feel that in order to pray, we have to be in a private room on our knees. But we must practice contacting the Lord at every time and under every kind of circumstance. We can speak to the Lord while we are walking on the street or while we are working or are busy with various matters. If we are about to lose our temper, we should tell the Lord, "O Lord, I am about to lose my temper." If we are about to criticize someone, we should say, "Lord, I am about to criticize." We must simply contact the Lord and tell Him everything, and then He will be our adjustment and correction. He will be the antibiotic to kill all the germs of our temper and criticism.

What does it mean to abide in the Lord? To abide in the Lord is to be in contact with the Lord all the time. It is not we who are living but it is the Lord who lives with us and in us in a practical way. As Paul says in Galatians 2:20, "It is no longer I who live, but it is Christ who lives in me." If we contact the Lord and receive Him as the life supply, He will revolutionize our entire life. For instance, suppose we intend to write a letter to someone, but before writing it, we contact the Lord and tell Him that we are going to write such a letter.

When we do this, the Lord will do something within us at that very moment, and consequently, the way in which we write the letter will be revolutionized. It will no longer be we who are writing the letter, but the Lord in us will be writing the letter. In every situation we can contact the Lord in such a way.

If we contact the Lord in this way, the Lord as the Spirit in our spirit will become the life supply to us, and we will be strengthened and refreshed. Furthermore, we will spontaneously know what to do, regardless of our situation, because the Lord will be living in us in a practical way. We will be living not by our natural life but by the Lord Himself, and we will be living another kind of life, a life not by ourselves but a life with the Lord. This is the life of the branch abiding in the vine (John 15:4-5). This is how to make real the mingling of God with man and the oneness of the Body. The more we contact the Lord and live by, through, and in Him, the more we will realize the oneness of the Body. The way to be truly one is not by exhorting each other to be united; rather, the way to be one is to contact the Lord in a living way moment by moment and to live in Christ. Then we will automatically and spontaneously be in the life of the Body and have the oneness of the Body. Whatever we do, we must contact the Lord first.

QUESTIONS AND ANSWERS

Question: Often I have found that after reading one or two verses, I cannot find anything in the verses over which to pray. In those instances, should I pray for other matters?

Answer: We should not make this practice of praying over the Word something legal. If you read a few verses without any understanding of them, how can you pray? You may have to read several verses or even half a chapter in order to understand something and be able to pray. The main thing is that instead of merely receiving the Word as knowledge with our mind, we must exercise our spirit to pray over the Word. We must exercise to contact the Lord with our spirit so that the Lord can be our life and life supply and so that we can carry out our daily living by this supply.

Question: Should we pray over the Old Testament as well

as the New Testament? It seems that it would be easier to pray over the New Testament because it clearly presents the different aspects of Christ, whereas in the Old Testament they are hidden.

Answer: This is a matter of the growth in life. A baby cannot take solid food; he must be given things that are easy to eat. Then when he grows older and stronger, he can eat the more solid food. As we practice to pray over the Word, we will grow in life and improve in our understanding of the Word. Eventually, we will realize that the entire Bible, including the Old Testament, reveals the riches of Christ. In fact, many verses in the Old Testament are even richer than those found in the New Testament.

Question: Is this kind of prayer something that you do only as an individual, or can it be done in a group as well?

Answer: First we should practice praying over the Word individually. Then we may be led to do this with some other saints. Eventually, we may advance to reading and praying with a large group in the meeting. It would be very good for the brothers and sisters to come together in a meeting to read the Word and then to pray over the Word. These prayers will touch our heart and saturate, strengthen, refresh, and illuminate our spirit.

What we lack today is a living contact with the Lord. We need to contact the Lord more than we need to read, study, and learn about spiritual matters. Our need is to contact the Lord Himself, because it is not Christianity or Christian teachings but the Lord Himself who is life and the life supply to us. Of course, if we are going to contact the Lord in a proper way, we must know about Him and study the Word. We surely need the proper teachings, but if we keep these teachings in our mind instead of using them for our prayer, they can damage us. Thus, our urgent need today is to constantly contact the Lord in our spirit.

Chapter Eight

THE PROPER FUNCTIONS OF THE SPIRIT, THE SOUL, AND THE HEART

Scripture Reading: 1 Thes. 5:23; Psa. 51:6; Jer. 31:33; Heb. 8:10; 4:12; Mark 12:30; Ezek. 36:26-27; 1 John 3:20-21; Heb. 10:22; John 16:22; 2 Cor. 11:3; Eph. 3:16-17

THE DISTINCTIONS BETWEEN THE SPIRIT, THE SOUL, AND THE HEART

If we want to contact the Lord and be mingled with Him, we must know the distinctions between the spirit, the soul, and the heart in more detail. First, we must be clear concerning the difference between the soul and the spirit. The teaching that the soul and the spirit are different is absolutely based upon the Holy Scriptures. First Thessalonians 5:23 says, "The God of peace Himself sanctify you wholly, and may your spirit and soul and body be preserved complete, without blame, at the coming of our Lord Jesus Christ." This verse mentions the three parts of man—the spirit, the soul, and the body. We all have an outward body, an inward soul, and a spirit, which is the innermost part of our being. Furthermore, the soul and the spirit are each composed of three parts. The soul is composed of the mind, the emotion, and the will (Psa. 139:14; S. S. 1:7; Job 6:7), and the spirit is composed of the conscience, the intuition, and the fellowship (Rom. 9:1; 1 Cor. 2:11; Eph. 6:18).

Regrettably, some Christians say that the soul and the spirit are the same thing and that the terms *soul* and *spirit* are synonymous. However, in 1 Thessalonians 5:23 there is the conjunction *and* between the words *spirit* and *soul,* proving that the spirit and the soul are not the same thing.

Furthermore, Hebrews 4:12 says, "For the word of God is living and operative and sharper than any two-edged sword, and piercing even to the dividing of soul and spirit and of joints and marrow, and able to discern the thoughts and intentions of the heart." This verse makes it clear that the spirit and the soul are two different things that can be divided from each other. This is not our concept; this is the teaching of the Scriptures. We must believe the Scriptures, not man's concept.

Hebrews 4:12 also mentions the heart, which refers not to the physical heart but to the psychological heart. What are the parts of the heart? First John 3:20-21 says, "Because if our heart blames us, it is because God is greater than our heart and knows all things. Beloved, if our heart does not blame us, we have boldness toward God." Inward condemnation is a function of the conscience, but these verses say that our heart can condemn us. This means that the conscience is a part of the heart. Hebrews 10:22 says, "Let us come forward to the Holy of Holies with a true heart in full assurance of faith, having our hearts sprinkled from an evil conscience and having our bodies washed with pure water." This verse also proves that the conscience is a part of the heart. John 16:22 says, "Therefore you also now have sorrow; but I will see you again and your heart will rejoice, and no one takes your joy away from you." Rejoicing and being happy are functions of the emotion. Thus, this verse indicates that the emotion is a part of the heart. Hebrews 4:12 mentions the "thoughts and intentions of the heart." Thoughts belong to the mind, and intentions belong to the will, indicating that the mind and the will are also parts of the heart. Thus, we may say that the heart is composed of four parts—the conscience of the spirit and the emotion, mind, and will of the soul. If we are going to know the Lord in the way of life, we must be clear about these matters. Otherwise, it will be difficult for us to be healthy Christians and to make progress with the Lord in the inner life. If a person wants to be a doctor, he must study the human body. Likewise, if we want to be healthy Christians, we must know the inward and hidden parts of our being.

THE FUNCTIONS OF THE HEART AND THE SPIRIT

The Word tells us that we must love the Lord (Deut. 6:5; Psa. 31:23). With what part of our being do we love the Lord? Mark 12:30 says, "You shall love the Lord your God from your whole heart and from your whole soul and from your whole mind and from your whole strength." There is no mention in the Scriptures of our loving the Lord with our spirit. In order to love the Lord, we must love Him with our heart, but in order to take the Lord, we cannot use our heart. For instance, suppose I offer you a book. No matter how much your heart loves the book, your heart does not have hands and cannot take the book. Suppose I give you an apple. No matter how much your heart loves the apple, it cannot eat the apple. You must use your mouth to eat the apple. Similarly, if we love the Lord and want to take Him in, we cannot take Him in with our heart. We must take in the Lord with our spirit (2 Tim. 4:22).

Ezekiel 36:26 says, "I will also give you a new heart, and a new spirit I will put within you; and I will take away the heart of stone out of your flesh, and I will give you a heart of flesh." This verse tells us that we have a new heart and a new spirit. The function of the new heart is to love the Lord, and the function of the new spirit is to receive the Lord. Sometimes we feel that it is sufficient to merely love the Lord without receiving Him. However, this is as foolish as thinking that it is enough to love our food and that it is unnecessary to eat it. We must eat our food and take it into us. Similarly, it would be foolish to merely love the Lord without taking Him into us. Loving the Lord is only the beginning; eventually, we must take Him in. We may love the Lord with our whole heart, but if we do not take Him in, we cannot gain Him.

Of course, we must first love the Lord with our heart in order to receive Him with our spirit. For instance, if there is good food on the table, but I do not have the appetite for it or do not like it, I will not take it. Thus, I first need a heart to love the food, but I also need the proper organ to receive it. I cannot take the food in through my eyes or ears. If I wanted to listen to someone's voice, I would use my ears, or if I wanted to look at some pictures, I would use my eyes. However, if I want to take in food and drink, I must use my mouth and stomach. Which organ of our being do we use to receive the Lord? We cannot use our ears, nose, mouth, eyes, hands, or even our mind to receive the Lord. If we want to understand some teachings, we need to exercise our mind, but it is impossible to receive the Lord with our mind, just as it is impossible to satisfy our hunger by meditating on food. We cannot use our heart to receive the Lord, even though we may love the Lord with all of our heart. We need to be clear that the organ we must use to contact and receive the Lord is our spirit.

EXERCISING THE SPIRIT

Our problem today is that although we may know how to love the Lord with our heart and how to read and meditate upon the Scriptures with our mind, we simply do not know how to exercise our spirit to take in the Lord. I have met many brothers and sisters who love the Lord very much, who read the Scriptures, and who can recite many verses. However, most of them do not know anything about taking the Lord in by using their spirit. We often use the wrong organ, trying to take the Lord in by using our heart or our mind. We must realize that the Lord is the Spirit and that the only way we can contact Him and take Him in is by using our spirit (2 Cor. 3:17; John 4:24). The part of our being that the Lord enters into is our spirit. Thus, we must know the difference between using the heart and using the spirit. In dealing with the Lord we must exercise to have a sincere, loving heart, but we also need to use our spirit. We must all ask ourselves whether we have had some experience of taking in the Lord by using our spirit.

Why is it that we may love the Word and be able to recite many verses, yet be unable to pray? This is because although our mind may be sharp and our heart may be proper, our spirit is weak and lacks exercise. Many Christians like to talk about the things of the Lord and to study the Scriptures, but when you ask them to pray, they become silent. They are happy and active in their mind and heart, but they are weak in their spirit. When we come together, our spirit should be active, living, and strong. Our spirit should be so strong, living, and active that we cannot waste time talking but must pray by using our spirit. Our situation today is abnormal; we use our mind and exercise our heart very much, but we neglect our spirit. We do not use it or exercise it, thinking that it is enough for us to understand the Lord and love the Lord. We must realize that even though we may love Him with our heart and understand Him with our mind, He may still be somewhat objective to us. If we want Him to be subjective to us, we must take Him in, receive Him, eat Him, and drink Him with our spirit.

In China I would often meet two kinds of Christians. One kind comprised the professors, medical doctors, and college students. They loved the Lord and studied the Word, and when you met with them, they would have many wonderful and interesting things to say about the Word. The professors would speak about the Bible from a scientific point of view, and the doctors would speak about the Bible from a medical point of view. However, if you asked them to close their books, close their eyes, and pray, they would become very quiet. On the other hand, sometimes I would go to a village to visit some saints who did not have much education. Some of the older women, even though they could not read, would pray all the time. You could not speak very much to them, because they would not understand, but if you asked them to pray, they would seize the opportunity. They were very active and living to pray aloud. The more I talked with those professors and doctors, the more deadened I became. However, the more I contacted those villagers, the more living I became, and the more my spirit was refreshed, satisfied, and strengthened. This proves that what we need is not only to love the Lord with our heart but also to exercise our spirit to contact and receive the Lord.

A PROPER HEART

The Scriptures tell us that our first need is a new heart (Ezek. 36:26a). If we do not have a heart that loves the Lord, nothing can be done. We also need a new spirit (v. 26b). We must exercise our heart to love the Lord and exercise our spirit to contact, take, receive, eat, and drink the Lord. While we are loving the Lord with our heart, we must exercise to contact the Lord with our spirit. However, if we are going to exercise our spirit to contact the Lord, our heart must first be adjusted; that is, we must have a proper heart.

We must be adjusted in the four parts of our heart in order to have a heart that is proper. First, we must have a pure conscience, a conscience without any kind of offense and without condemnation (Acts 24:16). We must be purified in our conscience (Heb. 9:14). This means that we must confess all our sins, trespasses, and faults (1 John 1:9). Our heart can never be right if there is a feeling of condemnation in our conscience. This will affect the ability of our spirit to contact the Lord in a proper way. Thus, we must deal with our conscience until it is pure and at peace.

Next, we must deal with our mind. Our mind must be simple. Second Corinthians 11:3 says, "I fear lest somehow, as the serpent deceived Eve by his craftiness, your thoughts would be corrupted from the simplicity and the purity toward Christ." The word *simplicity* refers to the simplicity of our mind toward Christ. If we have lost the simplicity of our mind toward the Lord, this is an indication that the enemy has corrupted our mind. We must be simplified in our mind. As Christians we are often complicated regarding spiritual matters. When we are asked whether we love the Lord, we may say, "Yes, I love the Lord, but..." If you ask the saints whether they would like to pray, they may say, "Oh, yes, but..." The brothers may say, "Yes, but I have to go to work." The sisters may say, "Yes, but I have to take care of the children." Everyone has an excuse. This is the complexity of the enemy. Do not say "but" to the Lord; say "no" to the enemy. Do not let your mind be corrupted by the enemy from the simplicity toward Christ.

Next, our will must be meek and soft toward the Lord. If our will is hard and unyielding toward the Lord, our heart will be wrong. If we have a stubborn will, our relationship with the Lord will be spoiled. We must have a will that is soft, submissive, and meek toward the Lord; then our heart and spirit will be proper.

Finally, our emotions must be full of love toward the Lord. The more we love the Lord the better. It would be best if we were beside ourselves with love for the Lord (2 Cor. 5:13-14). I am concerned that many of you have never been beside yourselves and are still more or less cold Christians. If you are a Christian, your heart must be so hot that you are beside yourself. Our conscience must be pure, our mind must be simple, our will must be soft, and our emotions must be full of love. This is a proper heart, the kind of heart that will be a help to our spirit in contacting the Lord.

After dealing with the four parts of our heart so that our heart is right and proper toward the Lord, we must exercise our spirit to contact the Lord. Then our spirit will be strengthened and satisfied, and our heart will be filled with the Lord and will become a home for the Lord. Ephesians 3:16-17 says, "That He would grant you, according to the riches of His glory, to be strengthened with power through His Spirit into the inner man, that Christ may make His home in your hearts through faith." When our heart has been adjusted and our spirit is exercised, our heart can be an abode for the Lord. We will be filled with the Lord in our spirit and our heart. The Lord will occupy our entire being and be formed in us until we are transformed and conformed to His image (2 Cor. 3:18; Rom. 8:29). This is real transformation—the mingling of God with us—and the issue of this mingling is the oneness of the Body. May we take care of these matters and practice them day by day.

Chapter Nine

TRANSFORMATION

Scripture Reading: Gen. 1:26-27; Col. 1:15; Rom. 5:14; 8:29; Gal. 4:19; 2 Cor. 3:17-18; Rom. 12:2; 8:6; 2 Cor. 2:16; Eph. 4:22-23; Col. 3:9-11; Eph. 2:15; Ezek. 36:26-27

MAN BEING A VESSEL OF GOD

The Bible tells us that man was created in the image of God and that the image of God is Christ (Gen. 1:26-27; Col. 1:15). This indicates that man was created according to Christ. Since this man, Adam, was created according to Christ, we may say that Adam was a figure or photograph of Christ (Rom. 5:14). Just as a photograph of you is according to you and is a figure of you, so Adam was made according to Christ and was a figure of Christ. However, there is no life in a photo. A photograph of you may be according to you, but it does not have your life within it. Likewise, Adam was made according to Christ but did not have the life of Christ.

Why was man created according to Christ but without the life of Christ? Man was created in this way because he was designated to be a vessel of God, a container for God (Rom. 9:21, 23; 2 Cor. 4:7). A container is always made according to its intended content. For example, a glove is made according to the image of a hand so that a hand can be put into it and become its content. The glove is a picture of man, and the hand is a picture of Christ, the embodiment of God. At the time he was created, Adam was made in the image of Christ, but he did not have Christ Himself as his life. Instead, Adam was given the free will to choose Christ as his life. Thus, after he was created, Adam was put before the tree of life, which typifies Christ, so that he could exercise his will to take the tree of life as his real life (Gen. 2:9). We must be very clear about this matter. Man is a vessel of Christ, a container for Christ. Without Christ we are nothing but an empty vessel. Since we were made to contain Christ, we must take Him in and be filled with Him (Eph. 3:19).

If a glove does not have a hand in it, it is nothing but an empty glove. If the glove could think and feel, it might wonder what it was made for or what the meaning of its existence is. However, if a hand enters into the glove, the glove will be filled and will feel that its existence is full of meaning. The real meaning of our human life is Christ; Christ is the content of our life. If we do not have Christ, we simply have emptiness and vanity (Eccl. 1:2). However, when we receive Christ as our life, He enters into us and fills us; consequently, our human life is filled with meaning.

THE MATTER OF TRANSFORMATION

God predestinated us to be conformed to the image of Christ (Rom. 8:29). In order to be conformed to the image of Christ, God first made us in the image of Christ and then caused us to believe in the Lord Jesus and receive Him as our life. Now we have both the image of Christ outwardly and Christ as life inwardly. However, there is still a problem. Although we have Christ within us, Christ has not yet been formed in us; in other words, we have not been transformed and conformed to the image of Christ very much (2 Cor. 3:18; Rom. 8:29). Christ is in us, He is living in us, and He is life to us in our spirit (Col. 1:27; Gal. 2:20; Col. 3:4; Rom. 8:10). However, Christ must be formed in us by the transformation of every part of our being. Through regeneration Christ became our life, and through transformation Christ will be formed in us (Gal. 4:19), and we will be conformed to the image of Christ.

Today in Christianity the word *transformation* is very much neglected. Christians talk much about sanctification (that is, positional sanctification), but they neglect the more important matter of transformation, which is a matter of life. Our nature and all the parts of our being must be transformed. We must realize that although we are vessels of Christ and

Christ is now in us as our content, our inward parts, which include our mind, will, emotion, and heart, may not be suitable for Christ to occupy, because they may be occupied by something other than Christ. Psalm 51:6 speaks of the inward parts, which are the parts of the soul, and of the hidden part, which is the spirit (1 Pet. 3:4). Christ as the Spirit is in our hidden part, our spirit (2 Tim. 4:22), but it is questionable whether or not He has the ground in our inward parts, the parts of our soul.

For example, a hand may enter into a glove, but it may not enter in all the way. The hand may be in the glove, but it may not be in all the fingers or parts of the glove. Christ is in us today, but how much is He in us? Christ is in us, but He has not yet been formed in us. He has been and is still being troubled by our soul. He has no peace and rest in our being, and as a result, we do not have peace and rest. This is the real condition of our relationship with Christ.

BEING TRANSFORMED
BY THE RENEWING OF THE MIND

We need to be transformed by the renewing of our mind (Rom. 12:2). Christ is now in our spirit, but He may not have much ground, room, or place in the other parts of our being, especially our mind. Our mind is the most important part of our inward being, because our daily life and our entire being are under the control of our mind. Sometimes it may seem that we are under the direction of our emotions, but it is actually our mind that directs our lives and our being. Thus, we must be transformed by the renewing of our mind so that we may be conformed to the image of Christ.

How can we be renewed in our mind? The Lord told us that anyone who wants to follow Him must deny himself (Matt. 16:24). The self is the natural life, and the most important aspect of the natural life, the self, is the mind (v. 23). Thus, to deny the self is primarily to deny the mind. If we are going to follow the Lord, we must deny our mind and the way we think. We may illustrate this matter in the following way. Recently I was traveling with an American brother who had an American mentality. After some time I began to think that, according to my traditional Chinese mentality, this brother was too modern. We went through some difficult times together, but eventually we realized that we should follow the Lord not by the modern American mind or the traditional Chinese mind but in and according to the spirit. If we are in our mind, we will not get along with one another, because in our natural mind we are individualistic and absolutely different from one another. However, there is no obligation for us to be subject to our mind. We can deny the soul-life and reject the natural mind by standing on the ground that we have been crucified on the cross (Rom. 6:6; Gal. 2:20). At the same time, we should exercise our regenerated spirit. If we deal with every situation in the spirit, the Lord will have the ground to subdue our natural mind, take control of our whole being, and fill our mind with Himself. In this way, our mind will be renewed.

One day I was very unhappy with a brother. The more I thought about him, the more I was displeased with him. However, at that moment I turned from my mind to my spirit and contacted the Lord in my spirit, saying, "Lord, forgive me for my thoughts about that brother." I denied my natural mind, gave up all my thoughts regarding that brother, and followed the Lord in my spirit. As a result, the Lord refreshed and strengthened me, and we were able to be together in the spirit. In this way the Lord occupied more of my mind. If we want to please the Lord and take Him as our life, we must learn the lesson of denying our mind in our daily life. Instead of being Christians who live in and according to the mind, we should turn from the mind to the spirit. We should not give any ground in our mind to the enemy; instead, we should let the Lord take over our mind and all the inward parts of our being. This is the only way for our mind to be renewed. By the renewing of the mind, our whole being will be transformed into the image of Christ.

In order for our mind to be renewed, we must also turn our heart away from everything else to the Lord. When we were regenerated, we received not only a new spirit with which to contact the Lord but also a new heart with which we can love God. Because of this, every Christian, whether he is newly saved or has been a believer for many years, has a longing to love the Lord. We must daily renew our love for the Lord. The enemy will often accuse us by injecting thoughts into our mind, saying, "How can a person like you love the Lord? You are too young and too weak!" We must deny and reject these thoughts, turn our heart to the Lord, and exercise our spirit to contact Him. Then the Lord will have the ground to expand Himself into all the parts of our being. This is the way to have our mind renewed and be transformed.

PUTTING OFF THE OLD MAN
AND PUTTING ON THE NEW MAN

We need to realize that the Lord is the Spirit, that we have a spirit, that this spirit was renewed at the time of our regeneration, and that the Lord Spirit is now living within our renewed spirit (2 Cor. 3:17; Job 32:8; Ezek. 36:26; 2 Tim. 4:22). We need to learn to deny the self and to turn from our mind to our spirit, from the outer man to the inner man. This is the reality of the putting off of the old man and the putting on of the new man in Ephesians 4:22-24. The way to put off the old man is by denying the self, and the way to put on the new man is by exercising the spirit. This is the way for our mind to be renewed and for our whole being to be transformed. In this way we are delivered from our old manner of living and transferred into the new man. When we are in the spirit, we are truly mingled with the Lord and are in the new man in a practical way. In the entire universe there is only one new man, and we are parts and members of that new man (Eph. 2:15; Col. 3:10-11). When we are in the new man, we are in the Body and have the oneness.

The way to realize the mingling of God with man and the oneness of the Body is first by regeneration and then by transformation. We have been regenerated, but we are still in the process of transformation. If we have been stopped or frustrated in this process, we must deal with all the frustrations and be transformed by the renewing of our mind so that the Lord may be formed in us and so that we may be conformed to the image of the Lord. Then we will be transferred from the old man into the new man and will be practically in the Body.

CHAPTER TEN

EXPERIENCING THE SPIRIT
INWARDLY AND OUTWARDLY

(1)

Scripture Reading: 2 Cor. 13:14; John 7:38-39; 20:21-22; Luke
24:49; 1 Cor. 12:13; Acts 1:5, 8; 2:1-4; Eph. 5:18

We have seen that the mingling of God with us is a matter
of our receiving the divine life and that oneness is a matter of
our being built up as the Body of Christ. Furthermore, we
have seen that oneness is the issue and expression of the
mingling of God with man. When we are mingled with God,
the oneness of the Body of Christ is automatically and spontaneously manifested among us. Both the mingling of God
with man and the oneness of the Body involve God being made
one with us. In order to be one with us, God as the Spirit came
into our spirit that we might be mingled with Him. It is in
this mingled spirit that we are one with God (Rom. 8:16;
1 Cor. 6:17).

BEING MINGLED WITH GOD
THROUGH THE FELLOWSHIP OF THE HOLY SPIRIT

The God in whom we believe is the Triune God; that is, He
is one, yet He is three. It is impossible to thoroughly understand this because it is far beyond our ability to comprehend.
However, it is a fact that our God is triune. He is one, yet He
is also the Father, the Son, and the Spirit (Deut. 6:4; Matt.
28:19). It may help to see how God is triune by using 2 Corinthians 13:14, which says, "The grace of the Lord Jesus Christ
and the love of God and the fellowship of the Holy Spirit be
with you all." This verse mentions the three of the Triune

God—God the Father, Christ the Son, and the Holy Spirit—and also three matters—love, grace, and fellowship. Love is of the Father, grace is of the Son, and fellowship is of the Holy Spirit.

How are the love of the Father, the grace of the Son, and the fellowship of the Spirit related to each other? Love is an inward matter; it is the hidden, intrinsic source within a person. For instance, suppose there is a brother whom I love. My love toward that brother is something hidden within me. However, suppose I present a gift to this brother. This is an expression of my love; my love for the brother is expressed through the gift. Thus, the expression of love is grace; grace is love expressed. Grace and love are actually two aspects of the same thing. They are like the two ends of a cord; what we see on one end is love, and what we see on the other end is grace. What is in the heart of God is love, but when the love of God is expressed to us, it becomes grace. John 1:17 says that grace "came through Jesus Christ," because Jesus Christ as grace is the expression of God and the expression of God's love (v. 18; 1 John 4:9). Love is the source within God, and grace is the expression of that love to us in the person of Christ. Thus, love is of the Father, and grace is of Christ.

When love is expressed, it becomes grace, but how does this grace reach us? This grace reaches us by the fellowship of the Holy Spirit, who is the transmitting substance. Love is in grace, and grace is in the fellowship. Love is the source, grace is the expression of the source, and fellowship is the trans-mission and realization of the expression with the source. God is love (vv. 8, 16), and we know God as love because He is expressed through Christ. Christ as the expression of God is grace to us, and this grace is the expression of the love of God. Furthermore, we can touch, experience, and realize this grace in the Holy Spirit and through the fellowship of the Holy Spirit.

The Father is the source, the Son is the expression of the source, and the Holy Spirit is the transmission and realiza-tion of the expression with the source. Because the Holy Spirit is in us, we can experience the Son and the Father, who is in the Son (Rom. 8:9-11). If we did not have the Holy Spirit, we would not have the Son, and if we did not have the Son, we would not have the Father, because the Father is in the Son (John 14:10), and the Son is the Spirit (2 Cor. 3:17). The three are one, just as love, grace, and fellowship are one. The Holy Spirit transmits everything that Christ is to us, and Christ is simply the expression of God Himself (John 14:26; 15:26; 16:13-14). Therefore, if we are going to apply Christ and be mingled with the Triune God, we must experience the Spirit. The only way we can touch and contact the Son and the Father, who is in the Son, is by the Spirit.

I am very burdened concerning our experience. What we lack is the experience of Christ, and the only way we can obtain, experience, and realize Christ is by experiencing the Spirit. If we are going to enjoy the love of God, we must have the grace of Christ, and if we are going to have the grace of Christ, we must have the fellowship of the Holy Spirit. It is in the fellowship of the Holy Spirit that we have the grace of Christ and the love of God. The love is in the grace, the grace is in the fellowship, and the fellowship is of the Holy Spirit. Thus, we must have the Holy Spirit.

BEING BORN OF THE SPIRIT, FILLED WITH THE SPIRIT, AND BAPTIZED IN THE SPIRIT

As Christians we already have the Spirit in our spirit (Rom. 8:16); if we did not have the Spirit, we would have neither Christ nor God. However, most of us have not experienced the Spirit in a full way. The best example in the Scriptures of one who fully experienced the Spirit is the Lord Jesus Christ. First, the Lord Jesus was born of the Holy Spirit. He was begotten in the womb of His mother Mary by the begetting of the Holy Spirit (Matt. 1:18, 20; Luke 1:35). Second, as He was being raised, the Lord Jesus was filled with the Holy Spirit. This is indicated by Luke 2:40, which says that the Lord Jesus was filled with wisdom, which is something of the Holy Spirit (Isa. 11:2). He was not only born of the Spirit; He was also raised in the Spirit and filled with the Spirit, and He walked and lived in the Spirit, as indicated by His caring for the things of the Father in Luke 2:40-52. He was a man of the Spirit.

We may think that it was sufficient for Him to be born of the Spirit and filled with the Spirit and to walk and live a life in the Spirit. However, when the Lord presented Himself at the age of thirty and was baptized in water, the heavens were opened to Him, and the Holy Spirit descended and came upon Him like a dove (Matt. 3:16; Luke 3:21-22). At the time of His baptism Jesus already had the Holy Spirit inwardly, yet the Holy Spirit still had to come upon Him outwardly. Thus, the Lord Jesus went through three steps in His experience of the Spirit: He was born of the Spirit, filled with the Spirit, and baptized in the Spirit. As genuine Christians we surely have been born of the Spirit. The Gospel of John tells us that when we were regenerated, we were born again of the Spirit (3:5-6). However, we also need to experience being inwardly filled with the Spirit (Acts 13:52; Eph. 5:18) and being outwardly baptized in the Spirit (Acts 1:5; 1 Cor. 12:13a).

THE TWO ASPECTS OF THE WORK OF THE HOLY SPIRIT

These three steps of our experience of the Spirit show us that the work of the Spirit has two aspects—the inward aspect and the outward aspect. The inward aspect consists of two steps—being regenerated and being filled. When we received the Lord Jesus as our Savior, the Spirit came into us to regenerate us, and since the day of our regeneration, He has been filling us with Himself. If we give Him the room and the ground in our being, He will fill every part of our being. Then we will be filled with the Spirit. These two steps are the inward aspect of the work of the Holy Spirit.

However, there is also the outward aspect of the work of the Holy Spirit. In the outward aspect the Holy Spirit comes upon us to clothe us, cover us, and baptize us. In the first aspect the Spirit is put *into* us, and in the second aspect the Spirit is put *on* or *upon* us (Acts 1:8; 2:17; 8:15-16; 10:44; 19:6). As Christians we have already experienced the first step of being born of the Holy Spirit. We may even have had some experience of being inwardly filled with the Holy Spirit. However, have we experienced being baptized in the Holy Spirit? We may have had some experience of the working of the Spirit within us, but have we had any experience of the working of the Spirit upon us? On one hand, the Spirit is the living water that we can drink (John 7:37-39; 1 Cor. 12:13b); on the other hand, the Spirit is like clothing that we can put on. Luke 24:49 likens the "power from on high," which is the Holy Spirit, to a piece of clothing with which we should be clothed. Inwardly, we must drink the Spirit; outwardly, we must be clothed with the Spirit.

We should not confuse these two aspects of the Spirit's work. Many Christians today are confused regarding the experience of the Spirit. Some say that being inwardly filled with the Spirit is the same as being baptized in the Spirit. However, the Scriptures clearly reveal that being filled with the Spirit and being baptized in the Spirit are two different aspects of the Spirit's work. First Corinthians 12:13 tells us that "in one Spirit we were all baptized into one Body" and that we were also "given to drink one Spirit." The drinking and the being baptized both involve the Spirit but in two different ways. To be baptized in the Spirit is to be put into the Spirit, just as to be baptized in water is to be put into water. However, to drink the Spirit is to take Him into us, just as to drink water is to take it into us. One cannot say that to be baptized in water is to drink water; similarly, we should not think that being baptized in the Spirit is the same as being inwardly filled with the Spirit. These are two different aspects of the Spirit's work.

THE APOSTLES' EXPERIENCE
OF THE HOLY SPIRIT

The Scriptures present to us not only the doctrine of the Holy Spirit but also several pictures of those who had the full experience of the Holy Spirit. The Lord Jesus was the first one to be born of the Holy Spirit, filled with the Holy Spirit, and baptized in the Holy Spirit. Later, His disciples followed His example in experiencing the Holy Spirit. In the evening of the day on which the Lord resurrected from the dead, the Lord came to His disciples and breathed into them, saying, "Receive the Holy Spirit" (John 20:22). Thus, on the day of resurrection Peter and the other disciples received the Spirit inwardly and were reborn with the eternal life. Later, the book of Acts tells us that the disciples were inwardly filled with the Spirit (13:52).

Although the Scriptures are clear regarding this matter, some Christians say that the disciples did not receive the Holy Spirit on the day of resurrection, but instead received Him on the day of Pentecost when the Holy Spirit came upon them. However, we must believe that when the Lord breathed the Spirit of the resurrection life into His disciples, they received the Spirit and were filled with the Spirit inwardly. We can prove this by comparing the disciples' condition before and after the Lord's death and resurrection. Before the Lord was crucified, the disciples, because of their pride, argued with one another about who was greater (Mark 9:34). However, after the Lord's resurrection and before the day of Pentecost, one hundred and twenty of them prayed together for ten days with one accord (Acts 1:14-15). Does this not prove that they were filled with the Holy Spirit? Without the inward filling of the Holy Spirit, it would have been impossible for one hundred and twenty of them to pray together for ten days without quarreling. The one hundred and twenty disciples gave up their countries, homes, and relatives and prayed together with one accord for ten days under the threatening of the Jewish authorities in Jerusalem. Surely this is proof that they had been filled with the Holy Spirit. Then Peter stood up and explained and expounded some of the prophecies in the Old Testament (vv. 16-20). This is another proof that he had been filled with the Holy Spirit before the day of Pentecost. Thus, we can see that the disciples were born of the Holy Spirit, filled with the Holy Spirit, and then baptized in the Holy Spirit (2:4).

There are several other examples in the Scriptures of people who experienced the Holy Spirit in the same way. One example is the believers in Samaria in Acts 8, who were born of the Holy Spirit when they believed the gospel preached by Philip (vv. 5-8, 12) and were later baptized in the Holy Spirit when Peter and John laid their hands on them to bring them into identification with the Body of Christ (vv. 14-17). Additional examples are the apostle Paul in Acts 9 (vv. 5, 11, 17-18) and the believers in Ephesus in Acts 19 (vv. 1-7). All these people went through the three steps of being born of the Holy Spirit, being filled with the Holy Spirit, and being baptized in the Holy Spirit. We must also experience these three steps. If we have not been born again, we have not yet been saved and are not yet children of God. If this is our case, we are Christians in name only; we have not been born of God and of the Holy Spirit. If we have been born of the Spirit, we may not have experienced drinking of the Spirit and being filled with the Spirit in such a rich and full way that the Spirit flows out of us as rivers of living water (John 7:37-39). We also may not have experienced being baptized in the Holy Spirit to be clothed with the Spirit. We should not merely listen to these words as we would listen to some doctrines. We must go to the Lord and check whether or not we have had all these experiences of the Holy Spirit.

By the Lord's mercy and grace, I can say that I have had all these experiences. One day in 1935 while I was ministering on the platform, I had a special experience of being clothed with the Spirit. According to my sensation, it was as if I had been immersed in a cloud and was in the cloud speaking. I could not see the cloud with my physical eyes, but I could sense it. While I was in that cloud, I was able to speak freely, and the whole atmosphere of the meeting changed. I had had the experience of being clothed with the Holy Spirit before, but that experience was the most impressive one.

There is an urgent need for us to experience the Spirit. Without experiencing the Spirit, we cannot experience Christ in a full and real way, because Christ is the Spirit. The Holy Spirit today is the Spirit of Christ, the Spirit of life, and the Spirit of reality (Rom. 8:9, 2; John 14:17). Apart from the Holy Spirit, Christ is merely a doctrine or knowledge in our mind. We must pray, ask, and seek that the Lord would grant us to experience the Spirit.

Prayer: Lord, we thank You that You are the Spirit in us. We thank You that You are no longer far away from us. Rather, You are so close and near to us because You are the Spirit in us. O Lord, we thank You that we can be filled with the Spirit and baptized in the Spirit. Thank You that we can be saturated and mingled with You as one. Lord, we look to

You to cause us to seek all these experiences, and we ask You to grant us all the necessary experiences of the work of the Spirit. We commit ourselves into Your hand that You may move and prompt our spirit and heart to seek, to pray, and to receive what You have given to us. We ask this in Your name. Amen.

CHAPTER ELEVEN

EXPERIENCING THE SPIRIT
INWARDLY AND OUTWARDLY

(2)

Scripture Reading: Eph. 5:18; Acts 13:52; 6:3, 5; 7:55; 11:24; Matt. 25:1-4, 8-9

We have seen that the mingling of God with man is a matter of the Spirit because the Triune God has been consummated as the Spirit. We have also seen that the work of the Spirit has two aspects—the inward aspect and the outward aspect. Thus, two different prepositions are used in relation to the work of the Spirit—*in* and *upon*. If we read the Scriptures carefully, we will notice that the Gospel of John mostly uses the preposition *in*, as in 14:17, which says, "The Spirit of reality...shall be in you." However, in the two books written by Luke, the preposition most often used in relation to the Spirit is *upon*, as in Luke 1:35, which says, "The Holy Spirit will come upon you," and Acts 1:8, which says, "You shall receive power when the Holy Spirit comes upon you." Thus, on one hand, the Spirit of God is working in us, and on the other hand, the Spirit is working upon us.

THE SPIRIT AS THE SUPPLY FOR OUR GROWTH
AND THE POWER FOR OUR SERVICE

The Bible often uses physical items to portray the Spirit. The two items that John uses to portray the Spirit are drinking water and breath (John 7:38-39; 20:22), which are vital for life. In order to live in the physical realm, we must breathe and drink. Similarly, in order to be normal Christians, we must breathe and drink the Spirit. The two items that Luke uses to portray the Spirit are clothing and wind (Luke 24:49; Acts 2:2-4). Clothing is something that we put on outwardly for authority (such as a uniform), and the blowing of the wind is also something outward for power, unlike breath, which is inward for life. These four items—water and breath, which are for life, and clothing and wind, which are for power— show us that we must pay attention to two matters—life and service. We must grow in the life of the Lord, and we must serve the Lord. Consequently, we have two kinds of needs. We need to be supplied that we may grow and mature in life, and we also need to be equipped so that we may serve the Lord. The Spirit meets both of these needs. On the one hand, the Spirit is within us as the life supply, and on the other hand, the Spirit is upon us to empower and equip us to serve the Lord.

In Matthew 25 there are two parables that pertain to the believers. One is the parable of the ten virgins (vv. 1-13), and the other is the parable of the talents (vv. 14-30). The parable of the virgins is on the side of life, and the parable of the talents is on the side of service. As virgins we must grow and mature in the divine life, and as servants of the Lord who have each been given a talent, we must use our talent in the best and fullest way. The growth in life and the use of our talent in our service depend very much on the two aspects of the Holy Spirit's work.

The Gospel of John deals with the matter of life, while the books written by Luke deal with the power needed in our service. The Gospel of Luke shows us that the Lord Jesus as the Savior preached and ministered to the people of the world by the power of the Spirit (Luke 4:14, 18; cf. Matt. 12:28). Similarly, the only way we can preach and minister the Lord to the worldly people so that people will receive Him is by the power of the Holy Spirit. If we are clothed with the Spirit, we will be able to preach the gospel to the entire world. Thus, at the end of the Gospel of Luke the disciples were told to wait until they were clothed with power from on high (24:49). In the book of Acts, also written by Luke, the power from on high came down upon the disciples, and they were filled and empowered with the Spirit to preach the gospel in a powerful way (2:2-4).

Many times the brothers and sisters wonder why it is so difficult to have good meetings or to pray to the Lord in the meetings. The reason is simply that many have not yet experienced the baptism of the Spirit. If we all experience the baptism of the Spirit, we will be released, and we will be equipped and empowered to carry out our service. I knew one brother who had such an experience in 1937. Before 1937 this brother had been saved and would pray privately in his own home, but he could not pray in the meetings or even sing the hymns. Then in 1937 Brother Watchman Nee came, and a number of brothers and sisters, including this brother, had the experience of being baptized in the Spirit. Immediately after that experience, this brother came to a meeting and offered a prayer. That prayer released the spirits of nearly all the saints that day. He was released, and others were released. From that day on, he opened his mouth to sing and to testify in the meetings. If we experience the baptism in the Spirit, we will be able to pray freely, to release our spirit, and to release others' spirits.

BEING FILLED WITH THE HOLY SPIRIT

We all have been regenerated by the Holy Spirit, and through our regeneration the Holy Spirit came into us and is now dwelling in us (John 3:6; Rom. 8:9, 11). However, the Word clearly indicates that after our regeneration we must be filled with the Spirit in every part of our being. In Acts "the disciples were filled with joy and with the Holy Spirit" (13:52). Joy goes together with the Spirit. If we are always unhappy, this indicates that we are lacking the Spirit. But if we go to the Lord in the morning and get freshly filled with the Holy Spirit, we will be full of joy. Acts 6:3 and 5 say, "Look for seven well-attested men from among you, full of the Spirit and of wisdom, whom we will appoint over this need....And the word pleased all the multitude; and they chose Stephen, a man full of faith and of the Holy Spirit." Furthermore, 11:24 says that Barnabas "was a good man and full of the Holy Spirit and of faith." These verses show us that faith and wisdom also go together with the Holy Spirit. If we are filled with the Holy Spirit, we will be full of joy, wisdom, and faith.

Matthew 25:1-4 and 8-9 say, "At that time the kingdom of the heavens will be likened to ten virgins, who took their lamps and went forth to meet the bridegroom. And five of them were foolish and five were prudent. For the foolish, when they took their lamps, did not take oil with them; but the prudent took oil in their vessels with their lamps....And the foolish said to the prudent, Give us some of your oil, for our lamps are going out. But the prudent answered, saying, Perhaps there will not be enough for us and for you; go rather to those who sell, and buy for yourselves." This parable is a warning to the foolish ones, the ones who are not filled with the Spirit. In this parable each virgin had a lamp. In the ancient days people did not have electric lamps; they had only oil lamps. In order for an oil lamp to be lit, there must be oil in the lamp. However, in addition to the lamp there is a vessel that holds extra oil so that when the light begins to go out, extra oil is prepared. Thus, there are two portions of oil. One portion is in the lamp, and the other portion is in the vessel. All of the virgins in this parable had their lamps lit; in this regard they were the same. The difference among them was in regard to the oil in their vessels. Five prepared oil in their vessels, and five did not. These five thought that as long as their lamps were lit, they were all right.

We must realize that each one of us has a lamp and that this lamp is our human spirit. Proverbs 20:27 says, "The spirit of man is the lamp of Jehovah." Since we have been regenerated, we have the oil of the Spirit in our spirit. However, we still must pay the price to prepare ourselves with additional oil in our vessel, which is our soul. In other words, although we have the Spirit in our spirit, we must be filled with the Spirit in our soul. To be filled with the Spirit is simply to grow and mature in the divine life. We have been regenerated, but have we grown and matured? If we are going to grow and become mature, we must be filled with the Spirit.

In order to be filled with the Spirit, we must first be emptied. Suppose we have a cup. If we want to fill this cup with tea, we must first empty out everything else that is in the cup. Likewise, we must check whether or not our being has been emptied. The Holy Spirit is in our spirit, but He must occupy our soul—our mind, emotion, and will. This is why the Bible uses the phrases *the mind of the Spirit* (Rom. 8:27) and *the spirit of your mind* (Eph. 4:23). The mind of the Spirit is a mind under the control and direction of the Spirit, and the spirit of the mind refers to a mind that is so full of the mingled spirit that the spirit has become the spirit of the mind.

In order to have the mind of the Spirit, we must first deny our natural mind. To deny the natural mind is simply to empty ourselves. We may be full of our own thoughts, the thoughts of the natural mind, so we must empty ourselves by denying the natural mind. Then the Spirit will take control of our mind and will occupy and fill our mind. As a result, our mind will be full of the Spirit, our mind will be the mind of the Spirit, and our spirit will be the spirit of our mind. The same thing must happen with our emotion and will so that every part of our being can be occupied and filled by the Spirit. Then the Spirit will be our constitution. Remember that the Spirit is the Spirit of Christ (Rom. 8:9-10). Thus, when the Holy Spirit occupies us, Christ occupies us, and when we are full of the Holy Spirit, we are full of Christ. When we are completely filled with the Spirit, we will be one with the Spirit and one with the Lord not only in our spirit but also in our soul. The Spirit of the Lord will saturate and be mingled with us in every part of our being. We will be mature and transformed in the divine life, and Christ will be formed in us (Gal. 4:19).

This matter of being filled with the Spirit cannot be accomplished merely by reading or listening to a message. We may read or listen to messages day after day for years, yet we may not be filled with the Spirit. There is only one way to be filled with the Holy Spirit: we must go to the Lord and contact Him by exercising our spirit. In other words, we must pray to the Lord (1 Thes. 5:17). The more we pray the better, because the more we pray, the more we exercise our spirit, and the more we learn how to give up ourselves and deny our natural mind. You may say, "I know that this is a matter of the cross"; however, it is not the knowledge of the cross that causes us to be filled but our contact with the Lord. By this kind of contact we will be able to give up ourselves and be filled with the Spirit.

CHAPTER TWELVE

EXPERIENCING THE SPIRIT INWARDLY AND OUTWARDLY

(3)

Scripture Reading: Luke 24:49; Acts 1:5, 8; 2:1-4, 13-18, 33, 36, 38-39; 10:44-47; 11:15-16; 8:14-17; 19:1-2, 6; 1 Cor. 12:3, 13

God's eternal purpose and ultimate intention are to mingle Himself with us for His corporate expression. We can experience this mingling because God is triune; that is, the Father is in the Son, the Son is the Spirit, and the Spirit as the very expression and realization of the Triune God can enter into us. If we miss the Spirit, we miss the entire Triune God. Thus, we must experience all the steps of the work of the Holy Spirit. First, the Spirit must enter into our spirit, which is the innermost part of our being, and regenerate us. This is our second birth (John 3:3-8). When we were born of our parents, we were born the first time, but when the Spirit enters into our spirit to regenerate us, we are born a second time. From this point on, the Spirit dwells in our spirit (Rom. 8:16). As we love the Lord and exercise our spirit to contact the Lord, we will realize that we must reject and deny our natural man, our soul-life (Matt. 16:24-25). Then the Spirit will strengthen and enable us to deny our self and will take more ground in our being. Consequently, we will be filled and saturated with Christ as the Spirit, and He will possess and occupy every part of our being. Christ will be our very element so that when we love, Christ loves in us; when we think, Christ thinks in our mind; and when we speak, Christ speaks through us.

We may think it would be good enough to be such a person. Yet if this were our condition, we would still be lacking something. We would be full of Christ inwardly, but outwardly we would still be somewhat short of Christ. However, once we experience being baptized and immersed in the Spirit—that is, being clothed with the Holy Spirit—we will be filled with the Triune God both inwardly and outwardly. We will have Christ as our life, our fullness, our power, and our covering. We will live in Christ, walk in Christ, and serve in Christ. As Christians we must be filled and saturated with the Spirit, and we must also experience being baptized in the Holy Spirit. We must have such experiences of the Holy Spirit in a definite way. Then Christ will be everything to us both inwardly and outwardly.

THE BAPTISM IN THE HOLY SPIRIT

In this message we would like to see something concerning the baptism in the Holy Spirit, or being clothed with the Holy Spirit. In order to see the need for the baptism in the Spirit, let us use the following illustration. Suppose there was a man who was full of food but was not adequately clothed. Such a man would be very abnormal. Inwardly, he would be full and satisfied, but his outward condition would be abnormal. In such a condition, he would not be able to do anything outside his house. From this we can see that with respect to the matter of life, it is sufficient to have Christ in us as our life, but for our service we must put on Christ as our clothing. If we were clothed but had nothing inside, our outward condition would be proper, but our inward condition would be abnormal. On the other hand, if we were full within but had nothing with which to cover ourselves, our inward condition would be satisfactory, but our outward condition would be abnormal. To be a normal Christian, we must be filled with Christ as life inwardly and clothed with Christ as power outwardly. We must live by Christ as our food and drink, and we must serve with Christ as our clothing to cover us. Then we will be fully mingled with Christ; Christ will be in us (Gal. 2:20), and we will be in Christ (John 15:4-5). This is what it is to be a normal Christian, one who is normal in life as well as service.

THE DIFFERENCE BETWEEN THE INWARD FILLING
AND THE OUTWARD FILLING

There are two different words in the Greek language for the word *fill*. The Greek word *pleroo* denotes the action of filling something within. The Greek word *pletho* implies the action of outpouring, of filling something outwardly. In the Greek language these two words are clearly distinct from each other, but in English they are both translated *fill*. In Acts 2:2 and 4 we see these two different words used. Verse 2 says, "Suddenly there was a sound out of heaven, as of a rushing violent wind, and it filled the whole house where they were sitting." The word for *filled* in this verse is a form of the Greek verb *pleroo*, indicating that the house was inwardly filled. Verse 4 says, "They were all filled with the Holy Spirit." The word for *filled* in this verse is a form of the Greek verb *pletho*, indicating that the disciples were outwardly filled with the Holy Spirit. Because the house in which the disciples dwelt was inwardly filled with the Spirit, the disciples were surrounded and outwardly filled with the Spirit. This is similar to our baptism in water. When we were baptized in the baptistery, which was inwardly filled with water, we were also filled with water. However, we were filled outwardly, not inwardly. Thus, to be baptized in the Holy Spirit is not an inward matter but an outward matter. Just as the water of baptism is outside of us and not inside of us, the Holy Spirit of baptism is outside of us and not inside of us. Inwardly, we must be filled with the Holy Spirit, but outwardly, we must be clothed with and immersed in the Holy Spirit.

FIVE CASES OF THE BAPTISM
IN THE HOLY SPIRIT IN ACTS

Let us consider the five cases of the baptism in the Holy Spirit in Acts. The first case occurred on the day of Pentecost when the one hundred and twenty disciples were baptized in the Holy Spirit (2:2-4). This was the fulfillment of the Lord's promise to His disciples in Luke 24:49 and Acts 1:5. The second case involved the believers in Samaria (8:14-17). There were a number of people in Samaria who had believed in the Lord Jesus, had been baptized into His name, and had received the Holy Spirit (vv. 12, 16b). However, these believers did not have the Holy Spirit upon them. Thus, Peter and John, two of the apostles, came down from Jerusalem to visit them. These apostles prayed that the Samaritan believers would be baptized in the Spirit (v. 15), and when they laid their hands on the Samaritans, the Holy Spirit came upon them (v. 17). Before their baptism in the Spirit, the Samaritans had the Holy Spirit within, because they had believed in the Lord Jesus, but they did not have the Spirit upon them.

The third case seen in Acts was the case involving Saul, who was saved on the way to Damascus (9:1-9). At that time he received the Lord as his Savior, the Spirit entered into him, and he was regenerated. The fact that Saul prayed to the Lord (v. 11) is an indication that he had been regenerated by the Lord. However, it was not until a disciple by the name of Ananias came to him, prayed for him, and laid hands on him that Paul was outwardly filled with the Holy Spirit (vv. 17-18).

The fourth case of the baptism in the Holy Spirit in Acts occurred in the house of Cornelius (10:44-46). After Peter spoke to those in Cornelius's house, the Holy Spirit came down upon them. Even though no one prayed for them or laid hands on them, they were baptized in the Holy Spirit. The fifth case involved the believers in Ephesus, who were genuine believers but had only been baptized into John's baptism (19:2-6). As believers, they had the Holy Spirit within them, but they did not have the Holy Spirit upon them. Thus, when the apostle Paul laid his hands on them, the Holy Spirit came upon them, and they were baptized in the Holy Spirit and clothed with the Holy Spirit.

With the first case there was no laying on of hands, because the Lord Jesus Himself baptized the disciples in the Holy Spirit on the day of Pentecost. The same thing happened in the fourth case in the house of Cornelius. Those in Cornelius's house were baptized in the Holy Spirit directly by Christ as the Head of the church. There was no need for an intermediary to lay hands upon them. Out of the five cases in Acts, only these two cases are referred to as the baptism in the Holy Spirit (1:5; 11:15-16). The other three cases seen in Acts are not called the baptism in the Holy Spirit. The reason for this is that the baptism in the Spirit, like the Lord's crucifixion, is an eternal fact. Just as all those who believe in the Lord Jesus have already been crucified on the cross (Rom. 6:6; Gal. 2:20), so also all those who believe in the Lord Jesus have already been baptized in the Holy Spirit. This is why 1 Corinthians 12:13 says, "In one Spirit we were all baptized into one Body, whether Jews or Greeks." The baptism in the Holy Spirit was fully accomplished on the day of Pentecost and in the house of Cornelius, and once it had been accomplished, it was accomplished forever and for every believer. The baptism in the Holy Spirit that occurred in Jerusalem was for the Jewish part of the Body of Christ, and the baptism in the Holy Spirit involving those in Cornelius's house was for the Gentile part of the Body of Christ. Thus, in these two cases both the Jewish and the Gentile believers are represented. Through these two events the Lord as the Head of the Body baptized the entire Body into the Spirit. This is why 1 Corinthians 12:13 uses the past tense in saying that we *were* all baptized in one spirit into one Body. The baptism in the Holy Spirit was the baptism into the Body and was for the Body.

EXPERIENCING THE BAPTISM IN THE SPIRIT BY REALIZING THE ONENESS OF THE BODY

We must realize that the baptism in the Holy Spirit is for the Body and not for individual believers. The eternal fact is that the Lord as the Head of the Body did not baptize individual believers in the Holy Spirit. Rather, He baptized His entire Body in the Holy Spirit on the day of Pentecost and at the house of Cornelius. If we examine the other three cases in Acts—the cases regarding the Samaritan believers, Saul, and the Ephesian disciples—we will see that in each case there was the need of the laying on of hands. Because the Body had already been baptized in the Holy Spirit, those who had been saved and had become members of the Body needed to realize the oneness of the Body in a practical way. They needed a representative of the Body to put his hands on them to signify that they had been received into the Body and had truly realized the oneness of the Body. When that representative laid his hands on them, the Head of the Body honored that by immersing them in the Holy Spirit, who was upon the Body. Thus, if we want to experience the baptism in the Holy Spirit, we must realize the oneness of the Body. If we remain individualistic and independent of the Body, it will be nearly impossible to experience the baptism in the Spirit. However, if we stand as those who have been joined to the Body of Christ, we will experience being clothed with the Spirit.

In Matthew 3:16 the Holy Spirit came down like a dove upon Christ, and this Christ is the Head of the Body. Thus, on the day of Pentecost and in the house of Cornelius the Spirit who had come down upon the Head also came down upon the Body. Now, whenever a person is saved, he needs to realize the oneness of the Body. If he sees the oneness of the Body and takes the oneness of the Body as his stand, he will experience the baptism in the Holy Spirit, because the anointing that is already on the Body will come upon him (Psa. 133:1-2). Thus, in order to have the experience of the baptism in the Holy Spirit, we must realize the oneness of the Body. We must tell the Lord, "Lord, I am standing on the ground of the oneness of the Body, and on this ground I claim the anointing that is on the Body." If we are truly on the ground of the oneness of the Body, we should simply claim the anointing that is already on the Body and take it by faith. We may tell the Lord, "Lord, I have the baptism in the Holy Spirit because I am in the Body, and the Spirit is on the Body. What is on the Body must also be my share, my portion."

THE BAPTISM IN THE SPIRIT BEING
A TESTIMONY OF THE LORD'S EXALTATION

We must also realize that the baptism in the Holy Spirit is a testimony of the Lord's exaltation. After the Lord Jesus ascended, He was exalted to the highest position in the universe and seated at the right hand of God (Acts 2:33a). He was made both Lord and Christ, as well as the Head of the church (v. 36; Eph. 1:20-22). People on the earth can know this by the outpouring of the Holy Spirit. On the day of Pentecost Peter told the people that the outpouring of the Spirit that they had witnessed was a testimony that Christ had been exalted. It was a testimony that Christ had ascended to the heavens, had received the promise of the Holy Spirit from the Father, and had poured Himself out as the Spirit upon the earth. Thus, whenever we are outwardly filled with the Holy Spirit, we will spontaneously say, "Jesus is Lord!" (1 Cor. 12:3b) because at that moment we will realize that this Jesus, who was put to death on the cross, has been exalted to the heavens, has been enthroned as Lord of all, and has been made the Head of the church.

After His resurrection the Lord came to His disciples and breathed into them, saying, "Receive the Holy Spirit" (John 20:22), and after His ascension He poured out the Holy Spirit upon His disciples like a strong wind to empower them that they might be a strong testimony to the world for Him. In His resurrection Christ dispensed Himself into us as the Spirit of life, and in His ascension He poured Himself out upon us as the Spirit of power. If we simply stand on the ground of the oneness of the Body, look to the ascended Christ, and claim what He has already poured out upon the Body by faith, we will experience the baptism in the Holy Spirit. After we experience the baptism in the Holy Spirit, we will realize that as members of the Body, it is our portion to serve the Lord. Many things, which only the Lord knows, will happen when we begin to serve. May the Lord be gracious to us that we may seek the infilling and the outpouring of the Holy Spirit and that we may be filled inwardly and clothed outwardly with the Holy Spirit. Then we will be normal Christians in life and service, those who are fully mingled with the Triune God and who enjoy all that God is to us and has for us.

ABOUT THE AUTHOR

Witness Lee was born in 1905 in northern China and raised in a Christian family. At age 19 he was fully captured for Christ and immediately consecrated himself to preach the gospel for the rest of his life. Early in his service, he met Watchman Nee, a renowned preacher, teacher, and writer. Witness Lee labored together with Watchman Nee under his direction. In 1934 Watchman Nee entrusted Witness Lee with the responsibility for his publication operation, called the Shanghai Gospel Bookroom.

Prior to the Communist takeover in 1949, Witness Lee was sent by Watchman Nee and his other co-workers to Taiwan to ensure that the things delivered to them by the Lord would not be lost. Watchman Nee instructed Witness Lee to continue the former's publishing operation abroad as the Taiwan Gospel Bookroom, which has been publicly recognized as the publisher of Watchman Nee's works outside China. Witness Lee's work in Taiwan manifested the Lord's abundant blessing. From a mere 350 believers, newly fled from the mainland, the churches in Taiwan grew to 20,000 in five years.

In 1962 Witness Lee felt led of the Lord to come to the United States, settling in California. During his 35 years of service in the U.S., he ministered in weekly meetings and weekend conferences, delivering several thousand spoken messages. Much of his speaking has since been published as over 400 titles. Many of these have been translated into over fourteen languages. He gave his last public conference in February 1997 at the age of 91.

He leaves behind a prolific presentation of the truth in the Bible. His major work, *Life-study of the Bible,* comprises over 25,000 pages of commentary on every book of the Bible from the perspective of the believers' enjoyment and experience of God's divine life in Christ through the Holy Spirit. Witness Lee was the chief editor of a new translation of the New Testament into Chinese called the Recovery Version and directed the translation of the same into English. The Recovery Version also appears in a number of other languages. He provided an extensive body of footnotes, outlines, and spiritual cross references. A radio broadcast of his messages can be heard on Christian radio stations in the United States. In 1965 Witness Lee founded Living Stream Ministry, a non-profit corporation, located in Anaheim, California, which officially presents his and Watchman Nee's ministry.

Witness Lee's ministry emphasizes the experience of Christ as life and the practical oneness of the believers as the Body of Christ. Stressing the importance of attending to both these matters, he led the churches under his care to grow in Christian life and function. He was unbending in his conviction that God's goal is not narrow sectarianism but the Body of Christ. In time, believers began to meet simply as the church in their localities in response to this conviction. In recent years a number of new churches have been raised up in Russia and in many eastern European countries.

OTHER BOOKS PUBLISHED BY
Living Stream Ministry

Titles by Witness Lee:

Abraham—Called by God	0-7363-0359-6
The Experience of Life	0-87083-417-7
The Knowledge of Life	0-87083-419-3
The Tree of Life	0-87083-300-6
The Economy of God	0-87083-415-0
The Divine Economy	0-87083-268-9
God's New Testament Economy	0-87083-199-2
The World Situation and God's Move	0-87083-092-9
Christ vs. Religion	0-87083-010-4
The All-inclusive Christ	0-87083-020-1
Gospel Outlines	0-87083-039-2
Character	0-87083-322-7
The Secret of Experiencing Christ	0-87083-227-1
The Life and Way for the Practice of the Church Life	0-87083-785-0
The Basic Revelation in the Holy Scriptures	0-87083-105-4
The Crucial Revelation of Life in the Scriptures	0-87083-372-3
The Spirit with Our Spirit	0-87083-798-2
Christ as the Reality	0-87083-047-3
The Central Line of the Divine Revelation	0-87083-960-8
The Full Knowledge of the Word of God	0-87083-289-1
Watchman Nee—A Seer of the Divine Revelation ...	0-87083-625-0

Titles by Watchman Nee:

How to Study the Bible	0-7363-0407-X
God's Overcomers	0-7363-0433-9
The New Covenant	0-7363-0088-0
The Spiritual Man 3 volumes	0-7363-0269-7
Authority and Submission	0-7363-0185-2
The Overcoming Life	1-57593-817-0
The Glorious Church	0-87083-745-1
The Prayer Ministry of the Church	0-87083-860-1
The Breaking of the Outer Man and the Release ...	1-57593-955-X
The Mystery of Christ	1-57593-954-1
The God of Abraham, Isaac, and Jacob	0-87083-932-2
The Song of Songs	0-87083-872-5
The Gospel of God 2 volumes	1-57593-953-3
The Normal Christian Church Life	0-87083-027-9
The Character of the Lord's Worker	1-57593-322-5
The Normal Christian Faith	0-87083-748-6
Watchman Nee's Testimony	0-87083-051-1

Available at
Christian bookstores, or contact Living Stream Ministry
2431 W. La Palma Ave. • Anaheim, CA 92801
1-800-549-5164 • www.livingstream.com